CW00505682

Level Seven
Core Book

CONSULTANTS: C. Burgess, L. Spavin, P. Thorburn

The Maths Quest programme is built on an
investigative approach in which knowledge is
constantly being used and applied. It adopts a topic
format which enables relevant parts of the National
Curriculum to be identified easily. It is the product of
real experience and has been compiled by a team of
teachers and advisers.

Schofield & Sims Ltd Huddersfield England

Contents

Blue Group used the picture of the Souvenir Shop to make up stories with missing words and numbers. They asked Gold Group first to work out what to do with each story and then to fill in the missing words and numbers.

> Addition and multiplication are about the same. You always have to find a total.

> If there are several different numbers you usually need to add.
> So Chris should add.

> So how do you decide which to do?

> But if all the numbers are the same then it's quicker to multiply. So Ali should multiply.

> If we already know the total and one part, and want to find a missing part, we subtract.

> Penny needed to subtract because 'change' is the missing part.

> When we split a starting amount into 2 or more equal parts, we divide.

> So Kim should divide.

a. Chris bought a ___ ___ and a ___ to give to his 3 visitors. What did he pay?

b. Ali bought 3 ___ to give to his friends. What did the gifts cost him?

c. Penny gave a £5 note to buy the ___. How much money did she get back?

d. Kim bought a pack of ___ postcards. What is the cost of one postcard?

e. Jim has £5 and wants to buy the ___. How much more does he need to save?

f. Fatima wanted to buy a bird poster. How much money would she need to save each week if she saved for ___ weeks?

g. Guy wants to buy ___ pencils to give to friends at his birthday party. What will all of the pencils cost him?

h. Bridget had ___. After she bought one gift she had ___ left. What did she buy?

---

1 **Copy out each story on this page.**

  a Write beside each story the operation you need to use.

  b Fill the gaps with items and prices from the picture of the Souvenir Shop.

  c Write each answer.

2 Use your own name and items from the picture to write a different story for each of these.

Subtraction		
795	870	2000
− 649	− 649	− 1485
___	___	___

Multiplication		
29	78	149
× 4	× 6	× 5
___	___	___

Division

6)96   5)660   5)875

3 Read your stories to others in your group.
Vote to see who wrote the clearest stories for each operation.

4 Write an approximate answer to each example in Question 2.

5 Calculate the exact answers for the stories you wrote in Question 2.

6 Use the picture to make up two more stories for each operation.

   a addition   **b** subtraction   **c** multiplication   **d** division

Sydney to Honolulu	8172 km
New York to London	5565 km
Glasgow to Zurich	1284 km
London to Paris	354 km
Warsaw to Athens	1601 km
London to Tokyo	12 697 km
London to Anchorage	7197 km
Moscow to London	2494 km

London to Johannesburg	9076 km
London to Athens	2404 km
London to Hong Kong	9622 km
Cardiff to Paris	502 km
Belfast to Paris	869 km
Athens to Moscow	2227 km
Sydney to Los Angeles	12 067 km
Anchorage to Tokyo	5541 km

Tokyo to Sydney	7825 km
London to San Francisco	8585 km
Sydney to Singapore	6302 km
New York to San Francisco	4139 km
Bahrain to London	5076 km
San Francisco to Honolulu	3857 km
Singapore to Bahrain	6327 km

1 Find out the distance for each flight*. Write each distance in both words and figures.

a London to Johannesburg   h Anchorage to Tokyo

b Cardiff to Paris   i Sydney to Honolulu

c Athens to Moscow   j London to Paris

d London to Hong Kong   k Glasgow to Zurich

e Sydney to Los Angeles   l London to Anchorage

f Belfast to Paris   m Warsaw to Athens

g London to Athens   n New York to London

2 Which flights match the numbers shown on these abacuses?

a 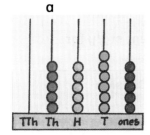 b 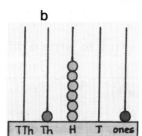 c 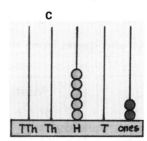 d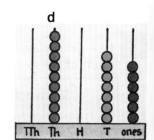

3 Write which flights in Question 1 are:

a less than 1500 km   b between 1500 km and 5500 km

c between 5500 km and 7250 km   d greater than 7250 km.

4 Write all of the flight distances in Question 1 in order from shortest to longest.

5 Round each flight distance in Question 1 to the nearest thousand kilometres.

6 Find out the distance from your home town to the capital of your country by air or road.

* The distances are also shown on *Stimulus Picture 1* for Maths Quest Level 7.

Melvin and Mary were helping their parents to work out the distance they had just travelled on their round-the-world trip.

Itinerary for Mr and Mrs Jones	
Sun. 7 October	depart London: arrive New York
Sun. 14 October	depart New York: arrive San Francisco
Sun. 21 October	depart San Francisco: arrive Honolulu
Sun. 28 October	depart Honolulu: arrive Sydney
Sun. 4 November	depart Sydney: arrive Singapore
Mon. 5 November	depart Singapore: arrive Bahrain depart Bahrain: arrive London

Use a calculator, paper and pencil wherever you need them.

7 Use flight distances rounded to the nearest thousand kilometres to work out the approximate distance of Mr and Mrs Jones's trip.

8 Melvin and Mary used a calculator to get the exact distance of the trip. What was the exact distance?

9 Here are some other trips to work out. Work out an approximate distance, then use the calculator to see how close you were to the exact distance.

    a Athens – Moscow – London – San Francisco – New York – London – Athens.

    b Sydney – Honolulu – San Francisco – London – Anchorage – Tokyo – Sydney.

    c London – Tokyo – Sydney – Singapore – Bahrain – London.

10 Make up some international trips that begin and end in each of these cities. Try to make each return trip as long as possible.

    a Moscow   **b** New York   **c** Sydney

The first railway in the world to carry passengers was the Stockton and Darlington Railway in eighteen twenty-five.

Jane's class made some charts about time.

1 **Write eighteen twenty-five in figures.**

    a What year was it one century later?

    b In twenty twenty-five how many years will have passed since the first railway in the world to carry passengers was opened?

The children looked up some important dates and wrote them on a time line.

2 **Use the time line to help answer these questions.**

    a How many years since Queen Elizabeth II was crowned?

    b How many years since man first walked on the moon?

    c How many years between the end of World War I and the beginning of World War II?

    d How many years did the Second World War last?

    e What year was the first cricket test played between England and Australia?

3 **Make a time line to show:**

    a the year you were born

    b the year of your tenth birthday

    c the year of your hundredth birthday.

4 **Write in figures the next ten years after the year two thousand.**

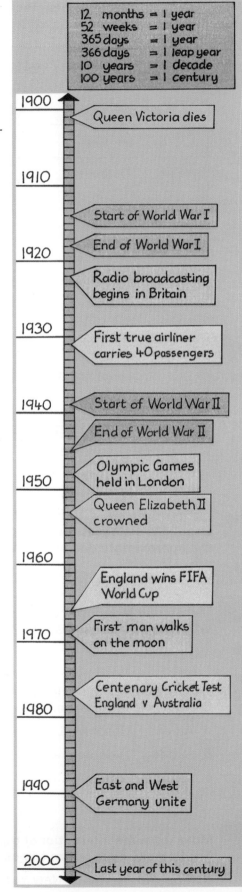

12 months = 1 year
52 weeks = 1 year
365 days = 1 year
366 days = 1 leap year
10 years = 1 decade
100 years = 1 century

1900 — Queen Victoria dies
1910
— Start of World War I
1920 — End of World War I
— Radio broadcasting begins in Britain
1930 — First true airliner carries 40 passengers
1940 — Start of World War II
— End of World War II
— Olympic Games held in London
1950 — Queen Elizabeth II crowned
1960
— England wins FIFA World Cup
1970 — First man walks on the moon
— Centenary Cricket Test England v Australia
1980
1990 — East and West Germany unite
2000 — Last year of this century

Tim said he would be staying at the beach for 70 days over the summer holidays.
His friends told him that their school holidays only lasted six weeks.

1 **Work out how many weeks there are in**

    a 70 days   **b** 35 days   **c** 21 days   **d** 49 days.

> To change days to weeks we divide by 7.

2 **How many days are there in:**

    a 4 weeks   **b** 8 weeks   **c** 6 weeks   **d** 9 weeks?

> To change weeks to days we multiply by 7.

Tina and Tony's holiday lasted 4 weeks and 6 days.

They converted the 'weeks and days' to days only.

Tina used pencil and paper.

Tony used a time line.

> $4 \times 7 + 6 = 34$ days

Tina
$$4w + 6d$$
$$\times 7$$
$$\overline{28d + 6d}$$
$$\overline{34 \text{ days}}$$

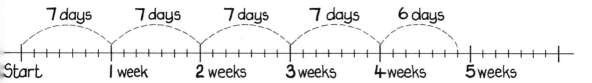

7 days   7 days   7 days   7 days   6 days

Start   1 week   2 weeks   3 weeks   4 weeks   5 weeks

3 **Express these 'weeks and days' as days:**

    a 13 weeks 2 days   **b** 16 weeks 1 day   **c** 13 weeks 4 days

    d 25 weeks 6 days   **e** 37 weeks 3 days   **f** 40 weeks 5 days.

Mandeep and Riaz had 38 days holiday.

They converted the days to 'weeks and days'.

Mandeep used pencil and paper.

Riaz worked it out in his head.

> $38 \div 7$ is 5 rem. 3 . . .
> 5 weeks 3 days

Mandeep
$$\begin{array}{r} 5r3 \\ 7\overline{)38} \\ 35 \\ \overline{3 \text{ days}} \end{array}$$

4 **Work out the length of these holidays in weeks and days:**

    a 16 days   **b** 70 days   **c** 30 days

    d 49 days   **e** 40 days   **f** 90 days.

5 **How many weeks and days are in one year? . . . one leap year?**

6 **Copy this table and fill it in.**

Use a calendar to help.

Time period	days	weeks and days
a. Winter season.		
b. Summer holidays.		
c. Schooldays in first term.		

The children made factor cards for each number along the top of the chart.

They were careful to stick their cards under the correct number.

1 Copy the chart. Make cards for every factor of each number along the top of the chart.

2 Use your chart to answer these questions:

a Which number is a factor of all numbers?

b Which number has exactly two factors?

c Which number on the chart is a prime number?

d Which number on the chart has the most factors?

e Which numbers on the chart have 4 as a factor?

f Which numbers on the chart have 5 as a factor?

3 Find all the common factors for these pairs of numbers.

a 4 and 6   b 8 and 20   c 20 and 75

d 50 and 75   e 75 and 100   f 25 and 100

'Common' means they are found in both numbers.

4 Write the common factor that is the highest for each pair of numbers in Question 3.

The common factor which is the greatest, is called the *highest common factor*.

We can also call the highest common factor the *greatest common factor*.

5 Find the highest common factor of each of these pairs.

a 6 and 20   b 5 and 50   c 12 and 75

d 8 and 25   e 12 and 100   f 75 and 100

6 Write 3 different pairs of numbers that have 10 as the highest common factor.

Mrs Young showed her group some fraction squares.

These fractions are all written in their lowest terms.

'Lowest terms' means that you can't find an equivalent fraction with a smaller denominator.

You can write 2 quarters as one half so $\frac{2}{4}$ is not written in its lowest terms.

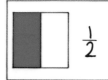 $\frac{1}{2}$

 $\frac{1}{3}$

 $\frac{2}{3}$

 $\frac{1}{4}$

 $\frac{3}{4}$

 $\frac{1}{5}$

Mrs Young now showed the group another fraction.

Is 8 twenty-fourths expressed in its lowest terms?

It doesn't look like it. Both 8 and 24 are high numbers for fractions.

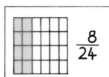 $\frac{8}{24}$

You need to be careful.

If you can divide **both** 8 and 24 by the **same** number, that means you can write the fraction in lower terms.

You won't always be able to find a lower equivalent fraction.

1 **Answer these questions about $\frac{8}{24}$.**

 a What factors are common to 8 and 24?

 b What is the highest common factor of 8 and 24?

 c Write $\frac{8}{24}$ in its lowest terms.

2 **Write fractions in their lowest terms for these pictures.**

a 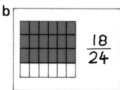 $\frac{16}{24}$

b 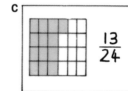 $\frac{18}{24}$

c 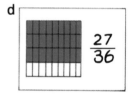 $\frac{13}{24}$

d $\frac{27}{36}$

How many steps did you need to find its lowest terms?

You can do it if you find the greatest number that divides both the numerator and the denominator.

That's the same as finding the *highest common factor* of the numerator and denominator.

3 **Write each of these fractions in their lowest terms.**

a 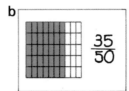 $\frac{16}{20}$

b 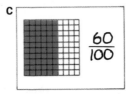 $\frac{35}{50}$

c 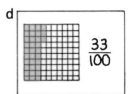 $\frac{60}{100}$

d $\frac{33}{100}$

Miss Lacy's class found out more about area.

Fred's group checked whether their desk tops measured more or less than one square metre.

1 How many square centimetres are there in one square metre?

2 Examine your desk top:

   a Estimate, then use the quickest method you know to measure the area.

   b Calculate how much more or less than 1 m² your desk top measures.

Les coloured some shapes on 1 cm² dot paper.

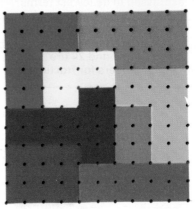

3 Write the area of these rectangles:

   a 4 cm × 3 cm   **b** 2 cm × 3 cm   **c** 6 cm × 2 cm.

4 Write the width of these rectangles:

   a area 12 cm²   **b** area 12 cm²   **c** area 6 cm²
   length 6 cm   length 4 cm   length 2 cm

One square represents 1 cm²

Next Les cut out and measured the shapes which were not rectangles. He noticed these could be separated into rectangles by a dotted line. This made it easy to work out the area of the whole shape.

You could make two rectangles from the shape.

Then you could add the two areas together.

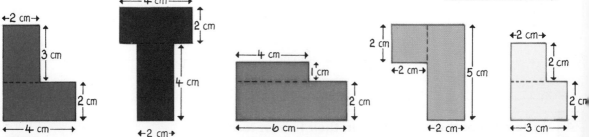

5 Use the measurements on each sketch to help:

   a Find the area of the separate rectangles.

   b Find the area of the whole shape.

6 Colour your own shapes on 1 cm² grid paper. Copy Les's idea.

Mike the gardener sometimes drew dotted lines on his plans to help him work out the area of paths, patios, lawns or flower beds.

1 **Look at the measurements for the paved areas sketched below.**

    a What unit would you choose to measure these areas?

    b Draw a plan of each area on dot paper*, then draw dotted lines where the plan can best be separated into two or three rectangles.

    c Use the measurements to help you work out the total area of paving needed for each job.

> Some plans have measurements missing . . . I can work these out from the other measurements.

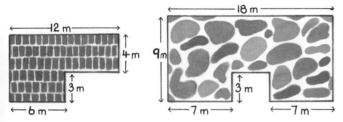

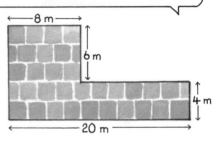

Sometimes Mike found it easier to enclose the whole plan in a rectangle and subtract the part that didn't belong.

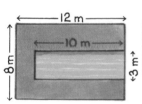

> (12 × 8) – (10 × 3) square metres of paving. That's 96 – 30 . . . 66 m².

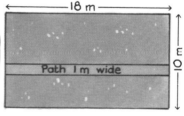

> (10 × 18) – (18 × 1) m² of lawn. That's 180 – 18 . . . 162 m².

2 **Use the measurements on these diagrams to help you work out the area of each coloured region.**

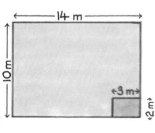

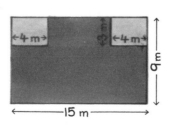

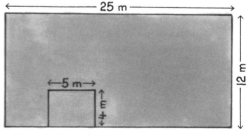

3 **Measure to the nearest metre the length and width of your class-room. Then draw a plan.**

    a Calculate the amount of carpet you would need to cover the whole floor.

    b Work out how much less carpet you would need if one corner is covered instead with a piece of lino 2 m × 1.5 m for a 'wet' area.

* Dot paper supplied on *Duplicate Master 5*.

Andy's class tried out different ways of making circles.

Jean and Greta used two pointed sticks joined with string to scratch a circle in the dirt.

The rest of the class made a closed curve around Olivia. They used a rope to measure how far away from Olivia to stand.

1 **Do what Andy's class did. How can you check whether you made a proper circle?**

> A closed curve can be called a circle if every point on the curve is the same distance from the centre.

Hold the top of the compasses . . . not the pencil.

2 **Try other ways of making a circle on paper.**

3 **Examine some drawing compasses.**

a Practise drawing circles with drawing compasses.

b Find out how to adjust the points so that you can draw larger or smaller circles.

c Use circles or part circles to make patterns.

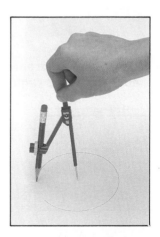

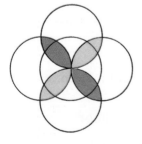 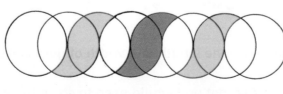

Try to keep the compasses upright.

Don't let the point slip.

4 Use your drawing compasses to draw three circles of different sizes. Then estimate, measure and record the distance from the curve to the centre of each circle.

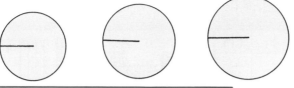

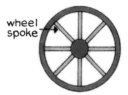

In Latin *radius* means 'a spoke'.

wheel spoke

The distance from any point on a circle to its centre is called the *radius*.

5 Use a ruler to help you adjust the points of your compasses so that you can draw different sized circles. Set your compass points to:

- 4 cm apart
- 5 cm apart
- 6 cm apart
- 7 cm apart.

a Draw circles each time.

b Measure the radius of each circle you draw.

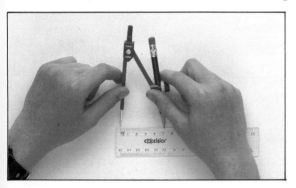

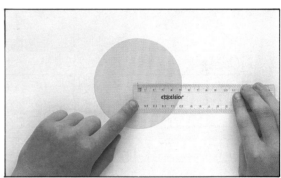

6 Cut out your circles and fold them in half. Then, estimate, measure and record the length of the fold across each circle.

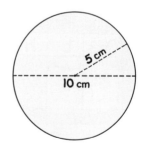

The distance across a circle, measured through the centre, is called the *diameter*.

Look! The diameter is double the radius.

7 Record the radius and the diameter of each circle you drew in Question 5. Draw more circles and record their measurements on the table. Can you see a pattern?

Our circles	
radius	diameter
4 cm	
5 cm	

Miss Jackson's class made a place-value chart to show numbers from thousands to thousandths.

They put base-ten blocks on the chart to show numbers.

The thousandths are very small.

This is three and four tenths.

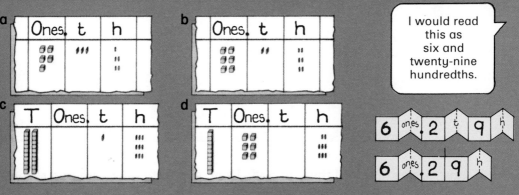

Th	H	T	Ones.	t	h	th

1 **Write each of these amounts in both words and figures.**

a | Ones. | t |

b | Ones. | t |

c | T | Ones. | t |

d | Ones. | t |

2 **Use a numeral expander to help you write these amounts in words and figures.**

a | Ones. | t | h |

b | Ones. | t | h |

c | T | Ones. | t | h |

d | T | Ones. | t | h |

I would read this as six and twenty-nine hundredths.

6 ones . 2 t 9 h

6 ones . 2 9 h

3 **Now use a numeral expander with thousandths to help write these amounts in words and figures.**

a | Ones. | t | h | th |

b | Ones. | t | h | th |

c | . | t | h | th |

d | . | t | h | th |

I read this as three hundred and seventy-five thousandths.

. 3 t 7 h 5 th

. 3 7 5 th

I could read this as three and forty hundredths
or
three and four hundred thousandths.

4 **Write each amount shown in Question 1 as hundredths and then thousandths.**

5 **Write each amount shown in Question 2 as thousandths.**

3 ones 4 t 0 h 0 th

When we measure the length of a ball throw, we can use tenths or hundredths of a metre.

This is three and sixty-five hundredths metres.

3.65m

1 Write each of these distances in words.

  a 3.6 m   b 7.6 m   c 7.1 m

  d 6.7 m   e 8.2 m   f 1.7 m

2 Write the distances in Question 1 in order from greatest to least.

3 Write each of these distances in words.

  a 2.36 m   b 7.91 m   c 7.08 m   d 8.15 m   e 6.92 m   f 7.19 m

When we compare a number with tenths to a number with hundredths, we still do it place by place starting at the greatest place value.

3.7m

3.65m

3.7 m is greater because it has more tenths.

4 Write all the distances in Questions 1 and 3 in order, from greatest to least.

5 Write each of these distances in words.

  a 3.265 m   b 5.995 m   c 6.955 m

  d 7.165 m   e 8.015 m   f 7.005 m

Sometimes we even measure length with thousandths.

6 Write all the distances from Questions 1, 3, and 5 in order from greatest to least.

7 Round all of the ball throw lengths in Question 6 to the nearest tenth of a metre.

8 Form a group to throw a ball.
   Each person should make 3 throws.

Bill's 1st throw	Bill's 2nd throw	Bill's 3rd throw
12.6 m	12.04 m	12.78 m

- Measure the first throw to the closest *tenth of a metre*.
- Measure the second and third throws to the closest *hundredth of a metre*.
- Record each measurement on a card.
- Sort the cards in order from greatest to least.

Ben's family bought an Italian family-sized pizza. Ben's dad asked him if he could work out his share of the cost.

PETE'S PIZZA PRICES

	MEDIUM	FAMILY SIZE
ITALIAN	£4·65	£6·80
CONTINENTAL	£5·95	£7·75
AMERICAN	£6·30	£9·45
THE 'LOT'	£8·20	£9·54
SUPER SPECIAL	£7·98	£9·82

Since we're splitting the cost equally, I'll need to divide.

There are 4 of us, so it's £6·80 divided by 4.

We divide the hundreds first.

Swap and then divide the tens.

And finally divide the ones.

```
      1
4)680
   4
   2
```

```
     17
4)680
   4
   28
   28
```

```
    170
4)680
   4
   28
   28
    0
    0
```

£1·70
4)£6·80

Each share is £1·70.

---

1 Work out the exact amount of each person's share.

   a 6 people share the cost of £7·98   **b** 5 people share the cost of £7·75

   c 7 people share the cost of £9·45

Sharon plays for a rounders team.

I know that I need to divide £9·45 by 9.

The nine players shared an American family-sized pizza.

Sharon offered to calculate each person's share of the cost.

The answer's a little more than £1 but I'll calculate exactly.

After I divide the hundreds there aren't enough tens to divide.

I must put a zero in the tens place, then I can swap the tens and divide the ones.

```
     1
9)945
   9
   04
```

```
    105
9)945
   9
   045
   45
```

£1·05
9)£9·45

Each person's share is exactly £1·05.

---

2 Work out the exact amount of each person's share of these pizzas.

Write an estimate first.

a 4 people share the cost of

£8·20

b 9 people share the cost of

£9·54

c 7 people share the cost of

£7·98

d 6 people share the cost of

£6·30

After the tennis match, the 6 players bought a medium-sized Italian pizza. Here is how they worked out how much each would pay.

3 Work out each person's share of the cost of these pizzas.

a 8 people share the cost of £9·82   b 6 people share the cost of £7·75

c 7 people share the cost of £9·54   d 8 people share the cost of £8·20

4 How much should each person pay for his or her share?

a 5 people shared a
£4·65 and a £6·30

b 8 people shared a
£9·54 and a £9·82

c 9 people shared a
£4·65, an £8·20 and a £7·98

d 10 people shared a
£4·65, a £5·95 and a £6·30

5 This is what Pete pays per kilogram for pizza-topping ingredients. Work out the approximate costs for each ingredient of:

a 100 g   b 125 g   c 200 g

d 250 g   e 500 g.

1 kg	cheese	£3·76
1 kg	tomatoes	£1·20
1 kg	ham	£7·56
1 kg	olives	£6·70
1 kg	salami	£5·45
1 kg	mushrooms	£4·32

6 What is the total cost of topping for each of these types of pizza?

ITALIAN
500 g cheese
125 g tomatoes
250 g ham

CONTINENTAL
250 g cheese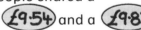
100 g olives
200 g salami

AMERICAN
125 g cheese
500 g ham
125 g mushrooms

Mr Hyde's class made up some problems during Health Food Week.

1 **Jim's group said "About how long is a bean?"**

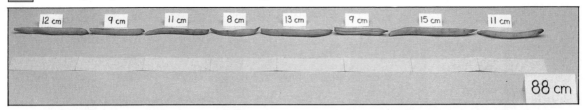

If we could join the eight beans together . . . then cut them into eight equal lengths . . . each bean would measure $\frac{1}{8}$ of 88 cm.

We did it with a paper strip . . . we found the average length of a bean is 11 cm.

a How did Jim's group find the average length of a bean?

b Copy their idea, using four beans in your experiment.

2 **Tessa's group each bought an apple.**

It's not fair! Your apple is heavier than mine.

We could find the average mass by weighing and dividing.

Then we can chop up all the apples and measure out five equal shares so we all get the same amount.

a What is the total mass of the group's five apples?

b How many grams would be in each equal share?

3 **Pat's group said "About how much juice is in an average orange?"**

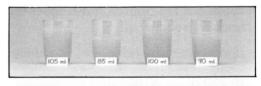

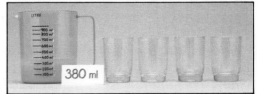

a Find the total amount of juice.

b How many oranges supplied this juice?

c What was the average amount of juice per orange?

per means 'for each'.

Jim wondered how many peanuts he could pick up in one hand.

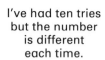

I've had ten tries but the number is different each time.

Let's show that on a graph.

I'd rather record it in a table.

Then you could work out the average.

OK. Show me how to do it.

Jim's Peanut Pick-ups

(Graph: Number of peanuts vs Number of tries, with peanuts plotted for 1st through 10th tries)

Peanut Pick-ups	
1 st	8
2 nd	11
3 rd	10
4 th	7
5 th	10
6 th	9
7 th	8
8 th	8
9 th	11
10 th	6
TOTAL	88

Jim

$$\begin{array}{r} 8.8 \\ 10\overline{)88} \\ \underline{80} \\ 80 \\ \underline{80} \\ 0 \end{array}$$

This doesn't come out evenly.

Well, 0.8 is close to another one, . . . let's approximate.

So . . . the average number is about 9.

1 **Look at the graph:**

 a How many tries did Jim have?

 b What was the total number of peanuts?

 c Why did Jim divide by ten?

 d Can you see how Jim's friend worked out the average number of peanuts in a handful?

We find the average by first adding all the scores. Then we divide the total by the number of scores.

The average tells how many there would be in each group if the total was shared evenly.

On the graph, Kay drew a line through the whole number that was closest to the average.

2 **How many of the handfuls contained:**

 a more than the average

 b less than the average

 c the average number?

3 **Form small groups and copy what Jim did. Use handfuls of peanuts or other small objects. If the numbers are large you could use a calculator.**

Jim's Peanut Pick-ups

4 **Look in newspapers, atlases or geography books for graphs showing average temperatures or rainfall. Talk about these.**

We already know what happens when we multiply tens by tens.

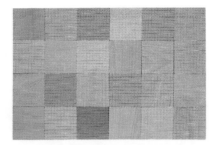

The base-ten blocks show 40 multiplied by 60

That's 24 hundred or 2400.

So tens multiplied by tens always gives hundreds.

We can often read hundreds as thousands and hundreds.

1 Write the answers in words as hundreds. Then write the answers in figures.

a	50	b	60	c	80	d	90	e	70	f	50	g	90
	× 70		× 60		× 70		× 50		× 90		× 80		× 90

Jack and Heather worked out the answer another way.

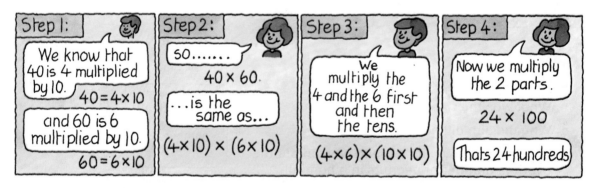

Step 1: We know that 40 is 4 multiplied by 10. 40 = 4 × 10 and 60 is 6 multiplied by 10. 60 = 6 × 10

Step 2: So....... 40 × 60. ...is the same as... (4 × 10) × (6 × 10)

Step 3: We multiply the 4 and the 6 first and then the tens. (4 × 6) × (10 × 10)

Step 4: Now we multiply the 2 parts. 24 × 100 That's 24 hundreds

2 Write each of the examples in Question 1 using Heather and Jack's steps. Write out the 4 steps for each example.

Jack and Heather tried a more difficult example.

We can think of 27 by 30 more easily by breaking up the tens part. 27 × (3 × 10)

We just multiply the 27 by 3. (27 × 3) × 10

Multiplying by 10 is easy because you just shift the digits along one place to the left. Don't forget to write the zero.

27 ×₂3 = 81   so   27 ×₂30 = 810

3 Copy these examples. Cover the zero in each example with your finger and multiply by the digit in the tens place.
Then complete the answer.

a	67	b	38	c	68	d	97	e	86	f	46	g	49
	× 20		× 30		× 40		× 50		× 60		× 70		× 80

Anna helped her dad work out how much he would get for selling all the grapefruit in a case.

We'll need to multiply 96 by 28.

96 GRAPEFRUIT — 28p each

We can do it in 2 parts.

96
×20
1920p

96
×8
768p

We add the 2 parts.

768p
+1920p
2688p

But it's quicker to do it like this.

96
×28
768
1920
2688p

That means the selling price for all the grapefruit in one case is £26·88.

---

1 Calculate the selling price for the fruit in each of these cases.

a 26p 84 kiwi fruit
b 25p 75 plums
c 34p 64 mangoes
d 19p 98 lemons
e 79p 36 avocados

---

2 These are the amounts that Anna's dad paid for the cases of fruit in Question 1. Calculate the profit that he made on each case.

a
1 case kiwi fruit
cost price
£15·35

b
1 case plums
cost price
£12·95

c
1 case mangoes
cost price
£13·50

d
1 case lemons
cost price
£9·90

e
1 case avocados
cost price
£17·50

The price paid by the shopkeeper is called the *cost price*.

---

3 The children held a fruit stall. Calculate the total profit they made on each kind of fruit.

4 What was the total profit for all the fruit the children sold?

5 How much more money do they need to make £50?

FRUIT SOLD		Number	Cost Price	Selling Price
	Delicious Apples	85	23p	35p
	Granny Smith Apples	94	17p	25p
	Pears	78	18p	29p
	Oranges	65	16p	30p
	250 g Bags of Grapes	35 bags	25p	40p

Freda and Jamil played a multiplication estimation game with a calculator.

Freda made up these examples.

Jamil used a calculator to find the answers but he wrote them in a different order.

Freda had to match each answer with its example.

a	b	c	d	e	f
79	49	36	72	49	57
x 69	x 31	x 26	x 63	x 38	x 85

| 936 | 1862 | 5451 | 4845 | 1519 | 4536 |

For the first one I'll round 79 up to 80, and 69 up to 70 and then multiply.

The answer will be a little less than 5600.

For the second one I'll round 49 to 50, and 31 to 30.

The answer must be close to 1500.

The third one is tricky since both ones digits are close to 5. I'll round 36 up and 26 down.

1 Use Freda's clues to choose the answers for the first three examples.

2 Work out the most likely answers for the last three examples. Each time, jot down how you made your estimate.

3 Calculate the exact answers to check all your estimates in Questions 1 and 2.

Here is another game that Jamil and Freda played.

Jamil's examples

a	b	c
39	97	54
x68	x82	x 36

d	e	f
81	75	67
x53	x 25	x 98

Freda's calculator answers

1875	6566
2652	7954
1944	4293

4 Jot down the estimates you would make to help match up Freda's answers with Jamil's examples. Then do the matching.

5 Calculate the exact answers to make sure that you did the matching correctly in Question 4.

Chris and Jim's mother bought a new video recorder and decided to pay for it over six months. She asked Chris and Jim to work out how much she would have to pay each month.

1 For each video recorder, write whether the answer will have only tens and ones, or hundreds, tens and ones.

a
£378
in 6 equal
monthly payments

b
£554
in 8 equal
monthly payments

c
£369
in 9 equal
monthly payments

d
£736
in 8 equal
monthly payments

e
£625
in 5 equal
monthly payments

Chris and Jim tried to make a closer estimate.

2 Write the two division examples you would use to make your estimate for each video recorder in Question 1. Then loop the example which gives you the closer estimate each time.

3 Write the two division examples you would use to estimate the answers for these. Then loop the closer estimate.

a 5 ⟌ 41 tens

b 6 ⟌ 41 tens

c 9 ⟌ 44 tens

d 8 ⟌ 44 tens

e 6 ⟌ 37 tens

f 8 ⟌ 29 tens

g 7 ⟌ 45 tens

h 9 ⟌ 60 tens

Suki's class examined things that turn.

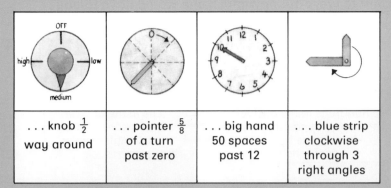

...knob $\frac{1}{2}$ way around	...pointer $\frac{5}{8}$ of a turn past zero	...big hand 50 spaces past 12	...blue strip clockwise through 3 right angles

Angles measure turns and part turns.

If something turns from one position to another, we say it turns 'through an angle'.

1 **Through how many right angles does the minute hand of a clock turn in:**

   a 15 minutes   **b** 45 minutes

   c 30 minutes   **d** 60 minutes?

2 **Measure in right angles:**

   a $\frac{1}{4}$ turn   **b** $\frac{1}{2}$ turn   **c** $\frac{3}{4}$ turn   **d** 1 complete turn.

The Ancient Babylonians believed that the sun took 360 days to travel once around the earth ... (What do we believe now?)

They divided one complete turn into 360 equal parts ... and called each part-turn 'one degree'.

We can write 'one degree' as 1°

Angles are measured in *degrees* ...

One complete turn measures 360°

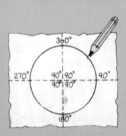

Suki folded a scrap of paper and marked the point where the folds intersected. Then she drew one full turn around the point she had marked.

3 **Use Suki's idea to find how many degrees the pencil passes through to make:**

   a a complete turn   **b** a quarter turn   **c** a right angle

   d a half turn   **e** 3 right angles   **f** four right angles.

4 Use a circle of cardboard, and a pointer which turns from the centre, to make an 'angle measurer'. Mark the circle in eighths, and number the scale from 0° to 360° so that each interval measures one eighth of a full turn.

a How many degrees does the pointer pass through to make $\frac{1}{8}$ of a full turn?

b Move your pointer clockwise from zero to show:
   ● 45° ● 90° ● 180° ● 270° ● 315°.

c Move the pointer clockwise from zero to measure:
   ● $\frac{4}{8}$ turn ● $\frac{1}{2}$ turn ● $\frac{1}{8}$ turn ● $\frac{3}{8}$ turn ● $\frac{5}{8}$ turn ● $\frac{7}{8}$ turn.

We use a ruler to measure lengths, but we use a protractor to measure angles.

5 Look at these home-made protractors. Do the numbers on the scale move clockwise or anticlockwise?

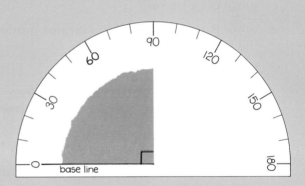

6 Look at these bought protractors. In which direction do you count:

a around the inside scale   **b** around the outside scale?

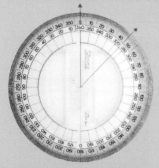

I measured a 45° angle.

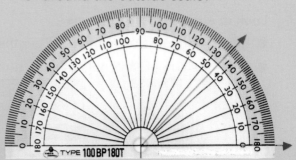

I measured another 45° angle.

7 Read the angle measurements shown on each of the protractors on this page.

8 Practise drawing angles and measuring them with a protractor.

Mrs Mitchell showed the children how to move
the turtle on the computer screen.

This is
the 'turtle'.

It does only
what you tell
it to do.

We can move
the turtle
forward 50
steps and then
back 50 steps.

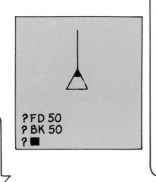

?FD 50
? BK 50
? ■

Now we can
turn the
turtle 90
degrees to
the right
and then
go forward
50 steps
and back
50 steps
again.

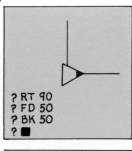

? RT 90
? FD 50
? BK 50
? ■

Pattern 1

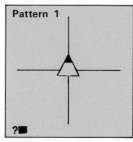

?■

Careful!
We must
get the
turtle back
to where
it started
from.

1 **The children kept the pattern going to make
'Pattern 1'.**

   a How much did they turn at each corner?

   b How many times did they turn to get the
   turtle back home?

   c What is the sum of all the angles made at
   the turns?

2 **Here are two more patterns the children
made. Answer these questions for 'Pattern 2'
and 'Pattern 3'.**

   a How much did they turn at each angle?

   b How many times did they turn the turtle to
   get it back home?

   c What is the sum of all the angles made at
   the turns?

Pattern 2

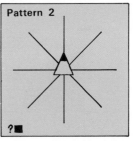

?■

Pattern 3

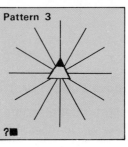

?■

3 **Look at each of these patterns.**

   ● How many turns were made to get the turtle back home?

   ● Write the size of the angle at each turn.

a

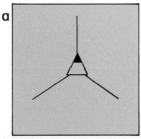

b

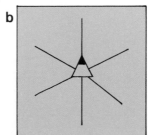

c

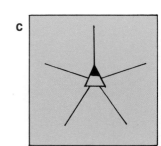

4 **Write instructions for making more angle patterns. The turtle must begin and
end at the start position each time.**

Jim and Judy were helping their father to work out how to fence a new paddock for their ponies.

We want it to be square.

We'll need to make the fence posts 5 metres apart.

Once we decide how big to make the paddock, we can work out how many posts to buy.

The children drew pictures to help work out how many posts they would need for square paddocks of different sizes.

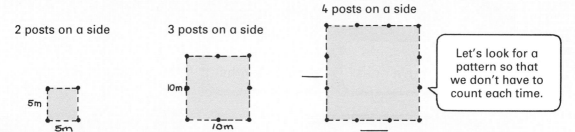

2 posts on a side

3 posts on a side

4 posts on a side

Let's look for a pattern so that we don't have to count each time.

1 **How many posts would they need if the paddock had 10 posts on each side? Discuss the different ways you could work it out.**
(There are 3 or 4 different ways.)

2 **Try different ways to work out how many posts they would need for a square paddock with:**

   a 100 posts on a side   **b** 500 posts on a side   **c** 1000 posts on a side.

3 **Write the dimensions (in metres) of the paddocks with:**

   a 10 posts on a side   **b** 100 posts on a side   **c** 500 posts on a side.

4 **Here are some triangular paddocks. Copy the table and use the pictures of triangles to help you complete it. Discuss all the different ways you could work out the missing numbers.**

2 posts on a side

3 posts on a side

4 posts on a side

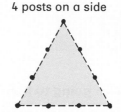

Can you see a quick way to do it for 1000 posts on a side?

Length of side	5 m	10 m	15 m					
Number of posts on a side	2	3	4	5	6	10	50	100
Total numbers of posts								
Total length of fencing								

Trevor, Sayeda and Claire each laid out lengths of string in the playground. Then they worked out the total length of each person's string.

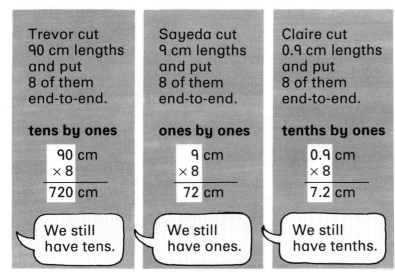

Trevor cut
90 cm lengths
and put
8 of them
end-to-end.

tens by ones

```
  90 cm
×  8
─────
 720 cm
```

We still have tens.

Sayeda cut
9 cm lengths
and put
8 of them
end-to-end.

ones by ones

```
   9 cm
×  8
─────
  72 cm
```

We still have ones.

Claire cut
0.9 cm lengths
and put
8 of them
end-to-end.

tenths by ones

```
 0.9 cm
×  8
─────
 7.2 cm
```

We still have tenths.

> When we multiply by ones we *don't* change the place values.

Back in the class-room, the children worked out what their totals would be if each laid out 80 lengths of string.

tens by tens

```
  90 cm
×  80
─────
7200 cm
```

ones by tens

```
   9 cm
×  80
─────
 720 cm
```

tenths by tens

```
  0.9 cm
×  80
─────
 72.0 cm
```

> When we multiply by tens we *do* shift the place values. We need to put in a zero to hold the place.

---

1 Copy these tables and fill in the answers.

a

	90	9	0.9
× 6			
× 60			

b

	90	9	0.9
× 7			
× 70			

2 Now keep the pattern going to hundredths. Copy the tables and fill in the answers.

a

	90	9	0.9	0.09
× 9				
× 90				

b

	60	6	0.6	0.06
× 8				
× 80				

Mr Gower needed to calculate the total mass of the load on his truck.
He asked Carol and John to help him.

1 **Calculate the total mass for each of these.**

a 25

b 48

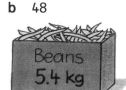

c 36

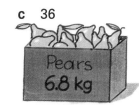

When we multiply with decimals, we use the same steps
as when we multiply without decimals. We need to
be careful about placing the decimal point in the answer.

2 **Calculate the total mass for each of these.**

Which examples have tenths in the answer?

a 36

b 36

c 25

d 25

Colin made a survey of the car colours in a car park. His teacher helped him display the information on a pie chart.

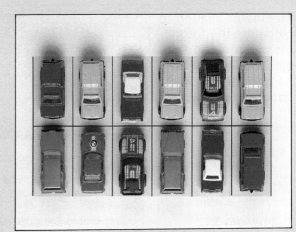

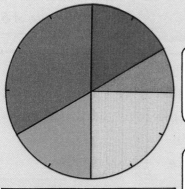

It looks like a pie cut into wedges.

I've worked out why you marked 12 equal intervals around the circle.

Yes, we call each wedge a *sector* of the circle.

Colours of cars in the car park.

1 **Use Colin's pie chart to help answer these questions about the cars.**

a Which colour is most popular?

b Which colour is least popular?

c What fraction of the drivers chose:
- yellow
- red
- green
- blue
- orange?

d Which two colours were equally popular?

e Which colours on the 'pie' cover:
- $\frac{1}{12}$ of the total
- $\frac{1}{3}$ of the total
- $\frac{1}{4}$ of the total
- $\frac{1}{6}$ of the total?

f Which two colours put together make up $\frac{1}{2}$ of the total?

2 **How many equal parts would you mark on the circle for a pie chart about:**

a 6 cars   b 10 cars   c 16 cars   d 24 cars?

John collects model cars.

3 **Cut out a circle of paper and fold it to make a pie chart about the cars in John's collection.**

a Paste the chart in your maths book and think of a title for it.

b Write at least one sentence about the chart.

	5kg Red Delicious £6·95
3kg Oranges £4·77	3kg Red Delicious £4·05
5kg Oranges £8·45	4kg Granny Smith £4·96

Lettuce	69p	
Carrots	89p	per kg
Tomatoes	£1·79p	per kg
Potatoes	47p	per kg
Onions	55p	per kg
Cabbage	39p	per kg
Grapes	£1·49p	per kg
Celery	79p	
Bananas	99p	per kg

The Ashley family always spend the same part of their weekly income on food. The other three families spend a different part of their income on food.

1 **Work out the amount each of these families budgeted for food.**

	Family	Weekly Income	Fraction to be spent on food
a	Ashley	£286	one-quarter
b	McDonald	£295	one-fifth
c	Baird	£312	one-eighth
d	Harvey	£354	one-sixth

We should budget to spend one quarter of our income on food each week.

This week our income is £286. We need to find one quarter of £286.

That's the same as dividing £286 by 4.

2 **Each of these families calculated how much out of their food budget they could spend on fruit and vegetables. Calculate how much they would have left to spend on other food items.**

a	b	c	d
Ashley £22·00	McDonald £25·00	Baird £25·00	Harvey £30·00

Each family buys fruit and vegetables from the same shop.
Here are their lists for one week.

a Ashley

2 lettuce
3 kg carrots
5 kg potatoes
5 kg cabbage
1 box Granny Smith
5 kg red apples

b McDonald

8 kg potatoes
6 kg cabbage
4 kg tomatoes
2 kg grapes
5 kg onions
3 kg oranges

c Baird

5 kg box oranges
5 kg red apples
2 celery
4 kg carrots

d Harvey

3 kg tomatoes
2 kg carrots
3 kg grapes
3 kg red apples
5 kg oranges

3 **Calculate how much each family will have left out of their fruit and vegetable budget.**

4 **If the surplus fruit and vegetable money is used for other food, how much will each family have left to spend on food altogether for that week?**

Liz and Arthur were trying to work out which bag of tomatoes was the better buy.

It would be good to work out the price for one kilogram in each bag of tomatoes. Then we'd see if the prices were the same or different.

Let's imagine we split up the 5 kg bag into 5 separate 1 kg bags. This is how we'd work out the price for each 1 kg bag: $5\overline{)695}$

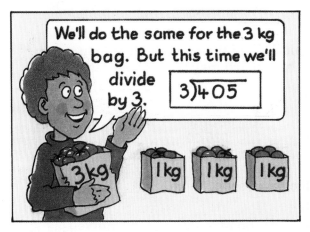

We'll do the same for the 3 kg bag. But this time we'll divide by 3. $3\overline{)405}$

Now we can compare the prices of the 1 kg bags in the two different lots.

1 Work out the price for:

   a 1 kg of tomatoes in the 5 kg bag   **b** 1 kg of tomatoes in the 3 kg bag.

> The price for buying one of any amount is called the *unit price*.

> The unit we used is 1 kilogram.

> We are working out the price per kilogram.

2 Compare the unit prices for the 5 kg and 3 kg bags of tomatoes. Which is the better buy?

3 Find the unit price for each of these. Then write which is the better buy for each pair of cases. (Use a kilogram each time as the unit.)

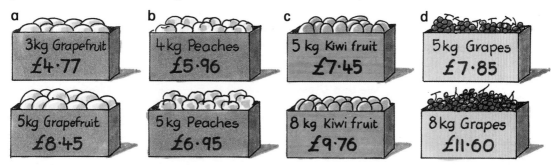

a 3kg Grapefruit £4·77 / 5kg Grapefruit £8·45

b 4kg Peaches £5·96 / 5kg Peaches £6·95

c 5 kg Kiwi fruit £7·45 / 8 kg Kiwi fruit £9·76

d 5kg Grapes £7·85 / 8kg Grapes £11·60

4 Write the name of the unit you will compare in each of these. Then decide which would be the better buy.

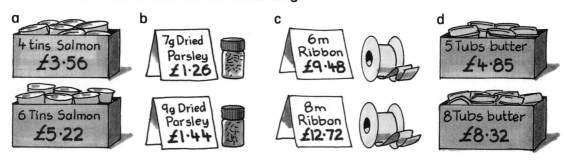

a 4 tins Salmon £3·56 / 6 Tins Salmon £5·22

b 7g Dried Parsley £1·26 / 9g Dried Parsley £1·44

c 6m Ribbon £9·48 / 8m Ribbon £12·72

d 5 Tubs butter £4·85 / 8 Tubs butter £8·32

Mrs Kingsley used to sell plums in 4 kg bags for £4·96.

She decided to sell them in 5 kg bags.

This is how she worked out what to charge for the 5 kg bags.

When I know the unit price, I can multiply that amount by 5.

$$4)\overline{496} = 124$$

$$124 \times 5 = 620$$

1 kg £1·24

This means I should charge £6·20 for a 5kg bag.

5 kg £6·20

5 Mrs Kingsley is going to charge the same unit price for each pair of cases. What price will she write on the bottom row of cases?

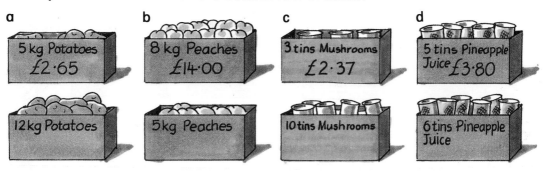

a 5 kg Potatoes £2·65 / 12kg Potatoes

b 8 kg Peaches £14·00 / 5kg Peaches

c 3 tins Mushrooms £2·37 / 10 tins Mushrooms

d 5 tins Pineapple Juice £3·80 / 6 tins Pineapple Juice

Kim and Lee showed how to write numbers using an Oriental system.

Our abacus has 5 in the hundreds place, 3 in the tens place and 6 ones.

When we write numbers in the Oriental system, we use these symbols to tell how many in each place.

Digit Symbols
1 is 一
2 is 二
3 is 三
4 is 四
5 is 五
6 is 六
7 is 七
8 is 入
9 is 九

The most important difference is that we also write the symbols for each place value that is greater than the ones.

Place-value Symbols
10 is 十
100 is 百
1000 is 千

We write five and hundred for five hundred

...and then three and ten for thirty.

五百三十六

We know the symbol without a place-value symbol means ones...

... six ones.

That looks easier than our system which is called the Hindu-Arabic system.

We wouldn't have to remember the place where each digit is written if we used the Oriental system.

1 Use the charts to help you to write these numbers using Hindu-Arabic symbols.

a 六百一十五　　b 六百七十二　　c 九十九　　d 四千一百三十五

There isn't a zero in the Oriental system!

2 How do you know which digit tells how many tens in:

a an Oriental number　　b a Hindu-Arabic number?

When there aren't any hundreds, tens or ones, you don't write anything for that sized group.

3 Write each of these numbers using Hindu-Arabic symbols.

a 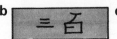 二十　　b 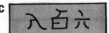 三百　　c 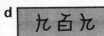 入百六　　d 九百九

4 Why do you need to be careful when you write a Hindu-Arabic number that doesn't have any hundreds, tens or ones?

Some of the children made cards to show multiplication and division by 10, 100 and 1000.

We know what happens when we multiply by 10, 100 or 1000.

If we cover the top factors we can work out what would happen if we divided by 10, 100 or 1000

28	28	28
× 1 0	× 1 00	× 1 000
28 0	28 00	28 000

× 1 0	× 1 00	× 1 000
28 0	28 00	28 000

28	28	28
1 0) 28 0	1 00) 28 00	1 000) 28 000

The children explored the pattern for another number and wrote what happened on place-value charts.

	HTh	TTh	Th	H	T	Ones
Start with					3	2
32 × 10				3	2	0
32 × 100			3	2	0	0
32 × 1000		3	2	0	0	0

When we multiply, the digits shift to the left.

When we divide, the digits get shifted to the right.

	HTh	TTh	Th	H	T	Ones
Start with			3	2	0	0	0
32 000 ÷ 10				3	2	0	0
32 000 ÷ 100					3	2	0
32 000 ÷ 1000						3	2

1 **Copy these tables and fill in the answers.**

a

Start with	99	145	12.5	0.9
Multiply by 10				
100				
1000				

b

Start with	99 000	145 000	12 500	900
Divide by 10				
100				
1000				

c

Start with	Multiply by				Divide by		
	1000	100	10	1	10	100	1000
1325							
5000							
875							
65							
9							

2 **Use a calculator to check your answers.**

Once a week, the pupils of Moorside school have swimming lessons at the local pool.

Some children saw this notice near the ticket box.

They wondered how much water was in a kilolitre.

> **Main Pool**
> **2000 kilolitres**
> **Diving Pool**
> **400 kilolitres**
> **Paddling Pool**
> **60 kilolitres**

1 **We use other measures that have names beginning with 'kilo'.**

   a How many metres equal one *kilo*metre?

   b How many grams are in one *kilo*gram?

   c How many litres do you suppose there are in one *kilo*litre?

| 1000 litres = 1 kilolitre |

> That's one thousand
> 1-litre cartons
> of orange juice.

2 **How many litres are in:**

   a 2 kilolitres   **b** 5 kilolitres   **c** 20 kilolitres   **d** $\frac{1}{2}$ kilolitre?

3 **How many litres are held in:**

   a the main pool   **b** the diving pool   **c** the paddling pool?

The children did a project on the history of measurement.

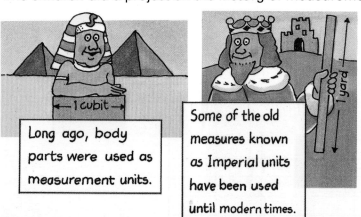

Long ago, body parts were used as measurement units.

Some of the old measures known as Imperial units have been used until modern times.

About 200 years ago all measurement units in France were changed to the metric system.

4 **Ask some adults what they remember about Imperial units.**

The children decided to find out more about measurement.

They made this table to show all the metric units they knew.

The Metric System

Larger units			Name of metric unit		Smaller units		
kilo						centi	milli
×1000	×100	×10		÷10		÷100	÷1000
kilometre			metre			centimetre	millimetre
kilolitre			litre				millilitre
kilogram			gram				

The larger units have Greek beginnings. The smaller units start with Latin prefixes.

In some countries they add these prefixes for the 'in between' measures.

hecto (100 units)
deca (10 units)
deci ($\frac{1}{10}$ unit)
centi ($\frac{1}{100}$ unit)

Equivalent Amounts

one thousand grams	one . . . . . .
one thousand metres	one . . . . . .
one thousand litres	one . . . . . .
one hundredth of a metre	one . . . . . .
one thousandth of a metre	one . . . . . .
one thousandth of a kilogram	one . . . . . .

1 Copy the chart on the right and use the Metric System table to help you complete it.

2 Convert these lengths to millimetres.

a 2 metres   b 3.5 metres   c 1.625 metres

3 Express the amounts shown on these packages in grams.

4 Write these capacities in millilitres.

a 1.625 litres   b 3 litres   c 2.5 litres   d 0.5 litres

5 Work out the capacity in kilolitres for these storage containers.

a water tank   b milk tanker   c oil tank

The hockey club bought cakes to sell on their stall. Each cake came divided into quarters, but they wanted to sell the cake in smaller pieces.

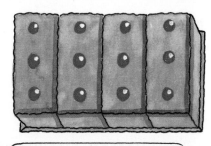

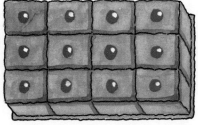

We could get 12 equal pieces because 12 is a multiple of 4.

Now we've got 12 equal pieces. So the size of one new piece is one twelfth.

It wouldn't be easy to get 10 equal pieces because 10 isn't a multiple of 4.

1 Write if it is possible to get these numbers of equal pieces from a block of cake that has been cut into quarters.

a 8   b 24   c 25   d 20   e 50   f 60   g 100

● Beside each answer explain what you did.

● Write the size of each new piece of cake as a unit fraction, e.g. $\frac{1}{12}$.

The hockey club divided all the blocks of cake into twelfths.

Three quarters of one cake was left over. How many twelfths was that?

To get twelfths we multiplied the denominator by 3. To get the *equivalent fraction* we must multiply the numerator by 3 as well.

Remember that the *denominator* is the bottom part of the fraction. The *numerator* is the top part.

2 Copy these and fill in the missing numerators to make equivalent fractions. (You can fold paper to help.)

a $\frac{1}{4} = \frac{\square}{16}$ b $\frac{1}{4} = \frac{\square}{32}$ c $\frac{1}{4} = \frac{\square}{80}$ d $\frac{1}{4} = \frac{\square}{100}$

$\frac{3}{4} = \frac{\square}{16}$ $\frac{3}{4} = \frac{\square}{32}$ $\frac{3}{4} = \frac{\square}{80}$ $\frac{3}{4} = \frac{\square}{100}$

Blue group made 'match cards' to show different ways they could write and describe hundredths that are greater than one.

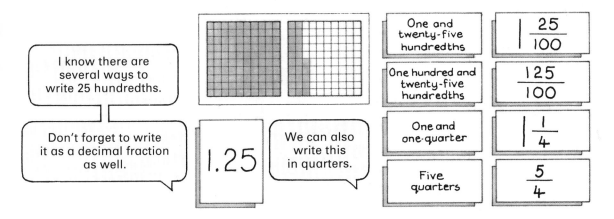

1   **Make all of the picture*, word and symbol cards for one and twenty-five hundredths.**

2   **Make all of the picture, word and symbol cards that match these pictures.**

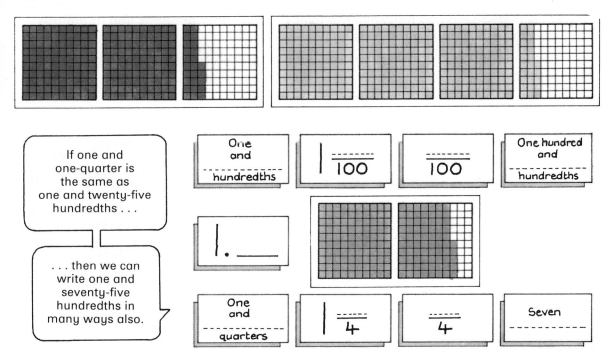

3   **Make all of the picture, word and symbol cards for one and seventy-five hundredths.**

4   **Make all of the picture, word and symbol cards that match each of these amounts.**

     a seventy-five hundredths   **b** two and seventy-five hundredths

     c one and one-half   **d** two and one-half

* Template for the picture cards is supplied on *Duplicate Master 29.*

Vera and Vince were given money to buy groceries.

The total price is about £2. I think I can get the exact price.

I'll add 128 and 40. That's 168. Then add 9. The exact total is £1·77.

I would do it another way. 128 plus 49 is the same as 127 plus 50. Yes, the total is £1·77.

1 Use Vera's or Vince's method to write an exact total for each of these pairs of purchases.

a 89p / 79p

b 27p / £3·48

c £1·26 / £1·29

d £1·98 / £1·24

e £2·35 / £1·36

2 Which method did you find easier to use? Discuss other methods you might use to get the exact total without using paper and pencil.

At the corner shop, Vince and Vera worked out the exact difference in price of breakfast cereals.

I'll count from 128 to 192 like this. 128 plus 2 is 130 . . . 130 plus 60 is 190 . . . 190 plus 2 is 192 . . . That gives a difference of 64p.

I'll add 2p to each price. That doesn't change the difference. 194 subtract 130 is 64 so we can get the answer easily.

3 Use Vince's or Vera's strategy to write the exact difference in price for these pairs of items.

a 83p / 37p

b £1·42 / 79p

c £1·85 / £1·39

d 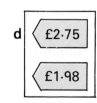 £2·75 / £1·98

e 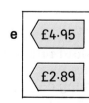 £4·95 / £2·89

4 Which subtraction method did you find easier to use? Discuss other methods you might use to get the exact answer without using paper and pencil.

The pupils needed to use a compass for orienteering. But first they made a direction card to practise with the points of the compass.

How to make a direction card
- Fold a square of stiff paper diagonally into quarters.
- Mark N S E W on the corners.
- Fold another square in the same way.
- Put a pin through the centre to help you position the two squares.
- Paste the first square on the second square.
- Mark the intermediate points – NE, NW, SE, SW.

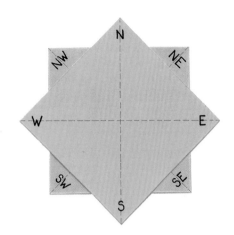

1 **Use the diagram to help you make your own direction card.**

a List the four cardinal points of the compass.

b List the four intermediate points of the compass.

2 **Use a real compass to locate the north boundary of your school's grounds. Mark it with a large label.**

a Stand on a chosen spot and line up your direction card with north.

b Make a list of the features you can see.

c Note the position of each feature in relation to your chosen spot.

> The big oak tree is east of the main entrance.

> The cycle shed is south of the main entrance.

3 **Use a protractor to measure the amount of turn between any two of the eight compass points.**

4 **Make up some direction games like this:**

a Face north. Turn right through 45°. What direction are you facing?

b Face north-east. Turn left to face west. Through how many degrees did you turn?

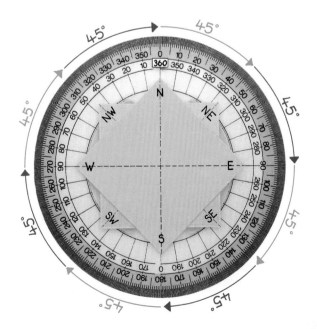

Miss Stacey's class was studying the population of the capital cities of the countries in the British Isles.

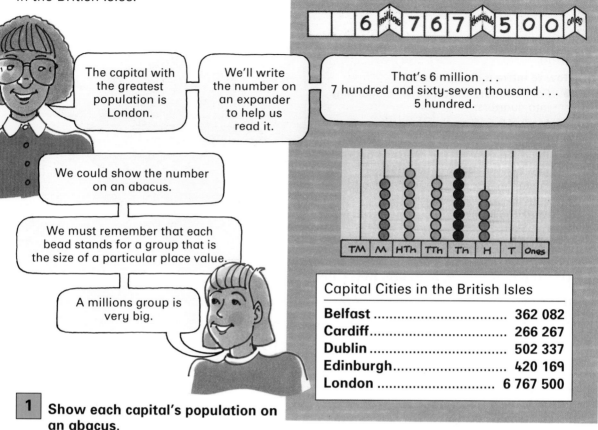

The capital with the greatest population is London.

We'll write the number on an expander to help us read it.

That's 6 million . . . 7 hundred and sixty-seven thousand . . . 5 hundred.

We could show the number on an abacus.

We must remember that each bead stands for a group that is the size of a particular place value.

A millions group is very big.

| TM | M | HTh | TTh | Th | H | T | Ones |

Capital Cities in the British Isles

Belfast	362 082
Cardiff	266 267
Dublin	502 337
Edinburgh	420 169
London	6 767 500

1 Show each capital's population on an abacus.

2 Write each population in words.

3 Copy this table and fill in the missing numbers.
What do you notice?

number	10	100	1000	10 000	100 000	1 000 000
one half of the number	5					
one quarter of the number	2.5					

4 **a** Write the names of the capitals in order of their population, beginning with the greatest population.

b Write the names of the capitals with more than half a million people.

c Write the name of the capital with the population nearest to quarter of a million people.

d Write the names of the two capitals with populations nearest to half a million people.

e Which capital has a population greater than all the other cities put together?

Mr Herd's class found this table showing the population of each country in the British Isles.

England	47 536 300
Northern Ireland	1 578 100
Republic of Ireland	3 540 643
Scotland	5 094 000
Wales	2 857 000

1 Use the table to write in words the population of each country.

2 Use the population figures for each country to calculate the total population of the British Isles.

3 The Republic of Ireland is not part of the United Kingdom. The four other countries make up the United Kingdom. Calculate the total population of the United Kingdom.

4 For each country, calculate how many people live outside the capital city. (Use the table on page 44.)

5 Which country has the greatest fraction of its population living in the capital city?

6 Which country has the smallest fraction of its population living in the capital city?

7 Write a list of the countries in the British Isles in order of their populations, beginning with the country with the smallest population.

The three third-year classes were dividing the profits from the school fête.

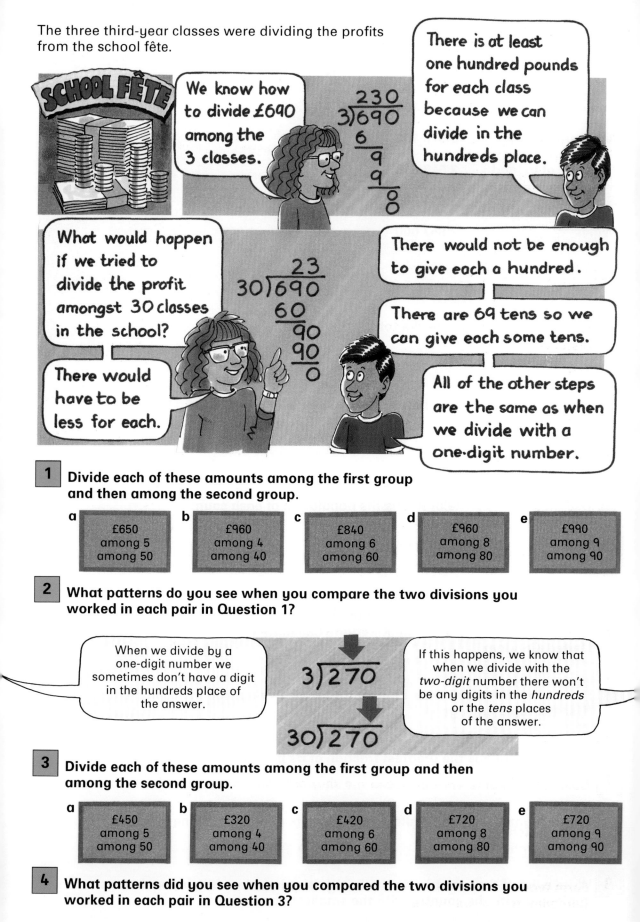

We know how to divide £690 among the 3 classes.

There is at least one hundred pounds for each class because we can divide in the hundreds place.

$$\begin{array}{r} 230 \\ 3\overline{)690} \\ 6 \\ \hline 9 \\ 9 \\ \hline 0 \end{array}$$

What would happen if we tried to divide the profit amongst 30 classes in the school?

There would have to be less for each.

$$\begin{array}{r} 23 \\ 30\overline{)690} \\ 60 \\ \hline 90 \\ 90 \\ \hline 0 \end{array}$$

There would not be enough to give each a hundred.

There are 69 tens so we can give each some tens.

All of the other steps are the same as when we divide with a one-digit number.

1 Divide each of these amounts among the first group and then among the second group.

a
£650
among 5
among 50

b
£960
among 4
among 40

c
£840
among 6
among 60

d
£960
among 8
among 80

e
£990
among 9
among 90

2 What patterns do you see when you compare the two divisions you worked in each pair in Question 1?

When we divide by a one-digit number we sometimes don't have a digit in the hundreds place of the answer.

$$3\overline{)270}$$

$$30\overline{)270}$$

If this happens, we know that when we divide with the *two-digit* number there won't be any digits in the *hundreds* or the *tens* places of the answer.

3 Divide each of these amounts among the first group and then among the second group.

a
£450
among 5
among 50

b
£320
among 4
among 40

c
£420
among 6
among 60

d
£720
among 8
among 80

e
£720
among 9
among 90

4 What patterns did you see when you compared the two divisions you worked in each pair in Question 3?

On Sports Day teams of three made running jumps. Each team member's jump was recorded and the team with the greatest total was the winner.

Teams	First jump	Second Jump	Third jump
Team 1	2.37 m	1.8 m	0.85 m
Team 2	1.2 m	1.02 m	2 m
Team 3	3.5 m	0.8 m	3.05 m
Team 4	3 m	1.75 m	0.9 m
Team 5	2 m	1.86 m	1.58 m
Team 6	1.9 m	3.7 m	0.95 m
Team 7	1.16 m	0.85 m	1 m
Team 8	1.2 m	0.65 m	1.15 m
Team 9	2 m	2.6 m	2.98 m
Team 10	0.97 m	3 m	1.62 m

1 What team do you predict has the greatest total?

When we calculate our total, we must make sure we line up the place values.

Team 1

T Ones . t h
```
  2.37 m
  1.8  m
 ₂0.₄85 m
 ------
  5.02 m
```

2 For each team, calculate the total distance jumped.

Which team had the greatest total?

3 Which teams had totals between 5.5 m and 5.05 m?

The record of 8.3 m for 3 jumps was set in 1991.

If we want to see how close we came to the record, we'll have to find the difference.

We'll also have to be very careful about lining up our place values when we subtract.

Team 1

T Ones . t h
```
  8.³⁰m
- 5.02 m
 ------
  3.28 m
```

4 Calculate how close each team came to the record.

5 Which teams were more than 3.5 m short of the record?

6 Calculate the range of the total results for all 10 teams.

7 Calculate the difference between the shortest and longest jump for each team.

8 Write which team had:
   a the smallest difference   b the greatest difference.

9 Form teams of 3 players. Make running jumps and record your results. Compare your team totals.

The local council fenced one hectare of parkland for athletics training. The fence measured 100 metres along each side.

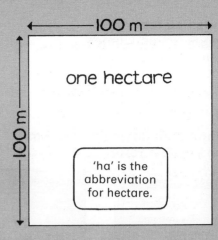

one hectare

'ha' is the abbreviation for hectare.

A square with sides 100 metres long has an area of *one hectare*.

1 How many square metres are in one hectare?

Jill's class used four 100 m lengths of string to enclose one hectare of their local park.

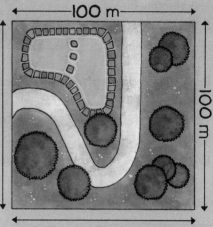

2 Try to mark out an area of about one hectare in your school's grounds or local park.

Melvin brought to school the plan for a new housing estate. The measurements for each house plot were marked on the plan.

3 Use Melvin's plan to help answer these questions.

   a What is the width of each plot?

   b What is the depth of each plot?

   c What is the area of each plot in square metres?

   d Write in hectares the total area of ten house plots.

   e What fraction of a hectare is each plot?

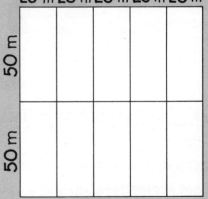

Paradise Gardens Housing Estate

4 Which areas are greater than 10 000 m² (one hectare)?

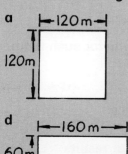

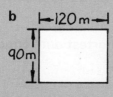

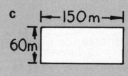

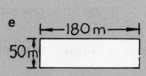

Helen and Tom's parents decided to buy a property in the country. They noticed that all the properties listed were measured in hectares.

1 **Look at the advertisements on this page.**

   a List the areas in order from smallest to largest. Then write the type of property beside each area.

   b Which property has an area of 300 000 square metres?

   c Which property has one half of the area of the Orchard?

2 **If the Caravan Park has a road frontage of 50 metres, what is its depth?**

3 **Work out the price per hectare for:**

   a the Dairy Farm   **b** the Market Garden Land

   c the Poultry Farm   **d** the Orchard.

4 **Work out the price of each separate lot of the Grazing Land. What is the price of the whole property?**

5 **What should the price of the Orchard be if it is:**

   a 16 ha   **b** 2 ha   **c** 6 ha?

6 **The Market Garden Land was sold to a developer who subdivided the land to make housing plots, each with an area of 1000 m².**

   a How many plots were made?

   b The total cost of putting in roads, water, power and sewerage was £450 000. For each plot, what were the developer's expenses for land and services?

Poultry Farm   **2 ha**
Houses 6000 hens   **£180 000**

Dairy Farm   **30 ha**
Rich pastures.
Sheds.   Asking **£210 000**

Caravan Park   **1 ha**
South Coast.
55 sites. House
and garden.   Price **£160 000**

Market Garden Land   **4 ha**
Superb water system.   **£145 000**

Profitable Orchard   **8 ha**
9–12 thousand cases pears,
apples, plums per annum.
Rich soil. Good brick home.
Packing room.
Cool rooms.   **£250 000**

Grazing Land   **120 ha**
As a whole or in 3 lots:
Lot 1   46.3 ha
Lot 2   40.9 ha
Lot 3   32.8 ha

    £1000 per hectare

Some travellers used the 24-hour clock system to work out their expected arrival time at the station nearest to their homes.

Traveller	Train departs	Time taken for journey	Expected time of arrival
Pat	08:20	2 h	
Judy	09:00	3 h 45 min	
Indira	10:05	6 h 20 min	
Ralph	10:40	2 h 30 min	
Sandip	13:10	8 h 50 min	

Pat and Ralph used a time line to work out their estimated arrival times.

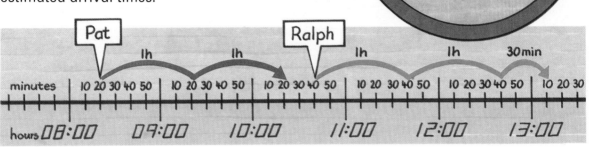

1 Make your own time line to show 24 hours. On your time line divide each hour into five-minute intervals.

> We'll use a different colour for each journey.

   a How many intervals will you show for each hour?

   b On your time line mark the train departure and arrival times for Judy, Indira and Sandip.

Judy and Sandip did a written calculation to work out their expected time of arrival.

	Judy	
h	min	
9	00	
+ 3	45	
12	45	

	Sandip	
h	min	
13	10	
+ 8	50	
22	00	

2 How did Sandip regroup sixty minutes? Use this method to work out the expected time of arrival for each traveller.

> 60 minutes . . . that's an hour.

3 Write the a.m. or p.m. time for the arrival of Sandip's train.

Train	Departs	Time taken for journey	Expected time of arrival
A	07:15	6h 25min	
B	11:25	4h 35min	
C	15:50	7h 15min	

> You can count on with a time line, or add up in columns.

4 Copy this timetable and work out the expected time of arrival for each train.

5 Make up a timetable for buses departing every 40 minutes from the airport and arriving 30 minutes later at the bus station in the city.

depart airport	arrive city
07:20	07:50
08:00	

The children began their annual Nature Trail walk at 09:30 hours. They strolled in small groups, observing plants, birds and animals along the way.

Group A returned to the starting point after $3\frac{1}{2}$ hours. Linda estimated they had spent 210 minutes on the trail. Thomas made a written calculation.

Linda
$3 \times 60 = 180$
$\frac{1}{2} \times 60 = 30$
_____
$3\frac{1}{2} \times 60 = 210$

| Thomas |
h	min
3	30
× 60	↓
180 min + 30min
Time 210 min

1 **Work out how many minutes there are in:**

a 2 hours   b 4 hours   c 5 hours   d 7 hours.

2 **How many minutes did each of these groups spend on the nature trail?**

● Group B
4 h 10 min

● Group C
2 h 50 min

● Group D
3 h 45 min

> To convert hours to minutes, **multiply** by 60.

3 **Work out what time each group arrived back. Show:**

a a.m. or p.m. time   b 24-hour clock time.

The children also took part in a walkathon.
Freda took 230 minutes to complete the course.
She estimated that this was a bit less than 4 hours.

Freda
$$
3
$$
$$
60\overline{)230}
$$
$$
-180
$$
$$
\overline{\quad 50 \text{ rem}}
$$
Time 3h 50 min

4 **How did Freda calculate her time in hours and minutes?**

5 **Work out how many hours there are in:**

a   120 minutes   b   240 minutes

c   480 minutes   d   600 minutes.

> To convert minutes to hours, **divide** by 60.

6 **Convert these times to hours and minutes.**

a 98 minutes   b 150 minutes   c 225 minutes   d 290 minutes

Mary and Clive help in their parents' computer shop. One of their jobs is to work out the prices of posting letters within the UK, and from the UK to the Isle of Man and the Channel Islands. They use this table to work out the prices.

Inland Letter Post

Prices shown refer to Royal Mail services within the UK and from the UK to the Isle of Man and the Channel Islands.

Mass not over	First Class	Second Class	Mass not over	First Class	Second Class
60 g	24p	18p	500 g	£1·20	93p
100 g	36p	28p	600 g	£1·50	£1·15
150 g	45p	34p	700 g	£1·80	£1·35
200 g	54p	41p	750 g	£1·95	£1·40
250 g	64p	49p	800 g	£2·05	No Second Class over 750 g
300 g	74p	58p	900 g	£2·25	
350 g	85p	66p	1000 g	£2·40	
400 g	96p	75p	Each extra 250 g or part thereof 60p		
450 g	£1·08	84p			

The Royal Mail aims to deliver (Monday to Saturday) first class letters the day after collection and second class letters the third working day after collection, but actual service depends on time of posting and the destination of the letter.

1 Use the table to work out the cost of mailing each of the following items:

Item	Mass	Class
a	40 g	2nd
b	398 g	1st
c	820 g	1st
d	590 g	2nd
e	235 g	2nd
f	1200 g	1st
g	1350 g	1st

2 Use your calculator to work out the total cost of mailing all the items in Question 1.

3 How much more would it cost if all the items in Question 1 were mailed First Class?

4 How much less would it cost if all possible items in Question 1 were mailed Second Class?

5 Mary and Clive had to work out the cost of mailing 65 letters, each with a mass of 75 g.

a What is the cost if all the letters are going First Class?

b What is the cost if all the letters are going Second Class?

c What is the total cost if 53 letters are going Second Class and the remainder First Class?

d Calculate the difference between the cost of the cheapest and the most expensive way of mailing the 65 letters.

Mary and Clive use this table to work out the cost of sending small packets to countries in Europe.

Small Packets to Europe		
Mass not over	Airmail	Surface Mail
100 g	62p	42p
150 g	82p	52p
200 g	£1·02	64p
250 g	£1·23	75p
300 g	£1·43	87p
350 g	£1·70	£1·06
400 g	£1·90	£1·15
450 g	£2·10	£1·26
500 g	£2·30	£1·36

6 Use the Small Packets table to work out the cost of mailing each of the following items.

Item	Mass	Airmail or Surface Mail
a	240 g	Surface
b	492 g	Airmail
c	90 g	Airmail
d	350 g	Surface
e	405 g	Surface
f	160 g	Airmail
g	360 g	Surface

7 Calculate the total cost of mailing all the items in Question 6.

8 How much more would it cost to send all the items in Question 6 by Airmail?

9 How much would be saved by sending all the items in Question 6 by Surface Mail?

10 Mary and Clive had to work out the cost of the following mailings:

a Twenty-four Second Class letters within the UK, each with a mass of 160 g, plus 13 small packets to Europe by Airmail, each with a mass of 430 g.

b Twelve small packets to Europe by Surface Mail, each with a mass of 205 g, plus 48 First Class letters within the UK, and 23 Second Class letters within the UK. Each letter has a mass of 275 g.

Brenda's class measured the perimeter of several things in their playground. They didn't have to measure every side of all the shapes.

3 m

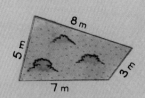

8 m
5 m
3 m
7 m

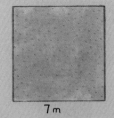

7 m

> I remember . . . the perimeter is the distance around something.

1 Use the measurements on the plans above to help you write the perimeter of each shape.

2 Discuss how you worked out the perimeter of those shapes that did not show the length of every side.

3 Use the measurements on the diagrams below to help you calculate the perimeter of each shape. Which is closest to a circular shape?

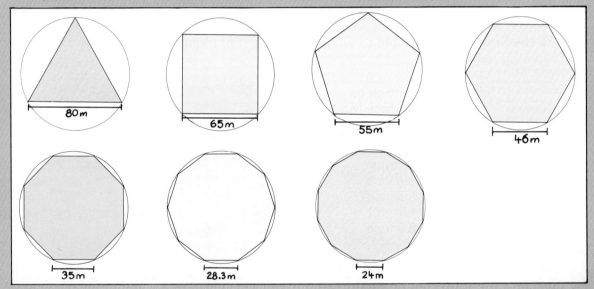

80 m

65 m

55 m

46 m

35 m

28.3 m

24 m

Ken wanted to measure the perimeter of a circle but he couldn't do it with his ruler.

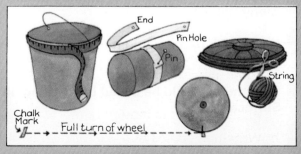

End
Pin Hole
Pin
String
Chalk Mark
Full turn of wheel

4 Try different ways of measuring the distance around a circular shape.

> The distance around a circle is called the *circumference*.

5 Estimate, measure and record the circumferences of circular shapes.

6 **What do we call these measurements?**

    a from the centre to the edge of a circle

    b across the widest part of a circle

    c completely around a circle

Brenda's class cut streamers to show the diameter and circumference of circular shapes.

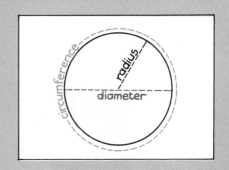

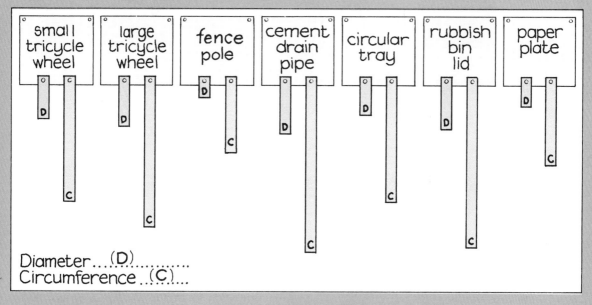

Diameter....(D)............
Circumference ...(C)....

This circumference is more than twice . . . no, it's a bit more than three times the diameter of the lid.

The diameter of this tray will fit along its circumference just over three times.

7 **Use your pencil as a measurer to find about how many times the diameter fits along the length of a circumference.**

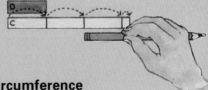

8 **Cut streamers to show the diameter and the circumference of some circular shapes in your class-room and in the playground.**

    a Compare the lengths each time to find how many times bigger one measurement is than the other.

    b Write a sentence about your results.

9 **Draw (with drawing compasses) and cut out a cardboard circle with a radius of 3.5 cm . . . 7 cm . . . 10.5 cm.**

    a Predict and measure the diameter of each circle.

    b Predict and measure the circumference of each circle.

Mr Morgan's class used grid paper to show area for regions of three different sizes. They coloured the region they wanted to show on each grid.

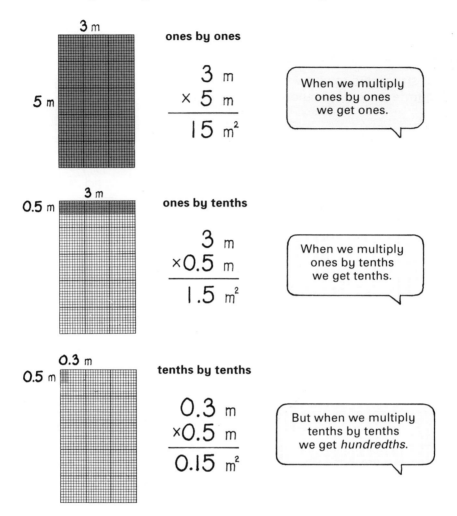

ones by ones

$$\begin{array}{r} 3 \text{ m} \\ \times\ 5 \text{ m} \\ \hline 15 \text{ m}^2 \end{array}$$

When we multiply ones by ones we get ones.

ones by tenths

$$\begin{array}{r} 3 \text{ m} \\ \times 0.5 \text{ m} \\ \hline 1.5 \text{ m}^2 \end{array}$$

When we multiply ones by tenths we get tenths.

tenths by tenths

$$\begin{array}{r} 0.3 \text{ m} \\ \times 0.5 \text{ m} \\ \hline 0.15 \text{ m}^2 \end{array}$$

But when we multiply tenths by tenths we get *hundredths*.

1 Copy this table and fill in the answers.
(You could use one-centimetre grid paper to help.
Let 1 centimetre represent one metre.)

a	b	c	d	e	f	g	h
7 m × 5 m	9 m × 7 m	8 m × 6 m	3 m × 6 m	8 m × 5 m	5 m × 4 m	3 m × 3 m	4 m × 2 m
7 m × 0.5 m	9 m × 0.7 m	8 m × 0.6 m	3 m × 0.6 m	8 m × 0.5 m	5 m × 0.4 m	3 m × 0.3 m	4 m × 0.2 m
0.7 m × 0.5 m	0.9 m × 0.7 m	0.8 m × 0.6 m	0.3 m × 0.6 m	0.8 m × 0.5 m	0.5 m × 0.4 m	0.3 m × 0.3 m	0.4 m × 0.2 m

2 Look at the table you have filled in.
What pattern do you see in the answers?

Mr Morgan's class coloured some more regions and looked for patterns in their answers.

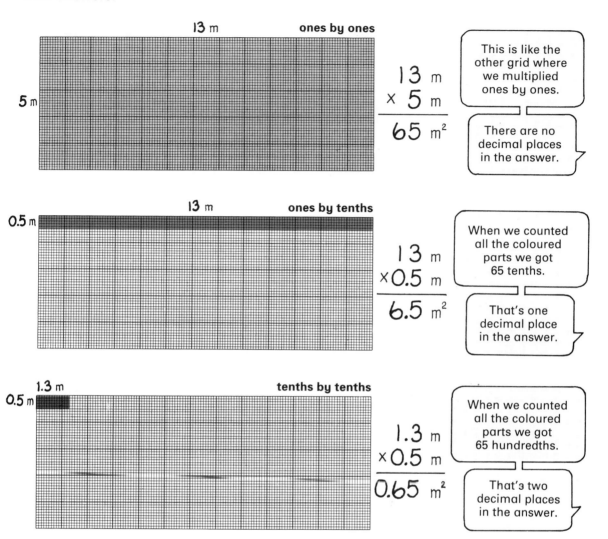

ones by ones

13 m

$\times$ 5 m

65 m²

This is like the other grid where we multiplied ones by ones.

There are no decimal places in the answer.

ones by tenths

13 m

$\times$ 0.5 m

6.5 m²

When we counted all the coloured parts we got 65 tenths.

That's one decimal place in the answer.

tenths by tenths

1.3 m

$\times$ 0.5 m

0.65 m²

When we counted all the coloured parts we got 65 hundredths.

That's two decimal places in the answer.

1 Copy this table and fill in the answers.

a 12 m $\times$ 3 m	b 24 m $\times$ 4 m	c 36 m $\times$ 3 m	d 32 m $\times$ 6 m	e 29 m $\times$ 8 m	f 31 m $\times$ 9 m	g 14 m $\times$ 5 m	h 25 m $\times$ 4 m
12 m $\times$ 0.3 m	24 m $\times$ 0.4 m	36 m $\times$ 0.3 m	32 m $\times$ 0.6 m	29 m $\times$ 0.8 m	31 m $\times$ 0.9 m	14 m $\times$ 0.5 m	25 m $\times$ 0.4 m
1.2 m $\times$ 0.3 m	2.4 m $\times$ 0.4 m	3.6 m $\times$ 0.3 m	3.2 m $\times$ 0.6 m	2.9 m $\times$ 0.8 m	3.1 m $\times$ 0.9 m	1.4 m $\times$ 0.5 m	2.5 m $\times$ 0.4 m

2 What patterns can you see on these two pages?

 Iskander and Jenny wanted to find the area of the rug in the staff room.

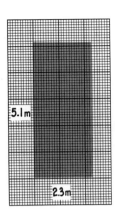

5.1 m

2.3 m

Let's draw the rug on grid paper.

That will give an idea of what our answer should be.

 We'll use the same steps as before.

  **We should set out this multiplication in the same way as the others we've been doing.**

$$\begin{array}{r} 5.1\ \text{m} \\ \times\,2.3\ \text{m} \end{array}$$

Step 1	Step 2	Step 3	Step 4
We'll start by multiplying by 3 tenths.	We could put in the decimal point here, but let's just remember that they're hundredths.	Now we'll multiply the ones and tenths by ones. That still gives us ones and tenths.	Now we can add the two numbers.
5.1 m .3 m	$$\begin{array}{r} 5.1\ \text{m} \\ \times\,2.3\ \text{m} \\ \hline 1\,5\,3 \end{array}$$	$$\begin{array}{r} 5.1\ \text{m} \\ \times\,2. \\ \hline 1\,5\,3 \\ 1\,0\,2 \end{array}$$	$$\begin{array}{r} 5.1\ \text{m} \\ \times\,2.3\ \text{m} \\ \hline 1\,5\,3 \\ 1\,0\,2 \\ \hline 1\,1.73\ \text{m}^2 \end{array}$$
We're multiplying ones and tenths by tenths. That gives us hundreths.	We'll put in the decimal point when we've finished.	We'll have to move the digits along to make sure they line up correctly.	There are tenths and hundredths in the answer, so it will have 2 decimal places.

1 Was the children's answer reasonable?

2 Calculate the coloured area on each of these grids.

a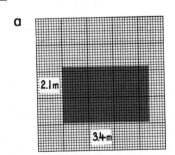

b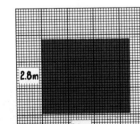

c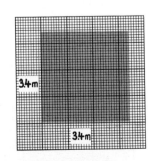

3 Draw each of these on grid paper. Then calculate the area.

a	6.2 m	b	2.7 m	c	2.8 m	d	3.0 m	e	2.8 m	f	3.7 m
	× 1.3 m		× 4.9 m		× 2.9 m		× 2.4 m		× 3.5 m		× 0.9 m

Iskander decided to check their answer with their drawing of the rug.

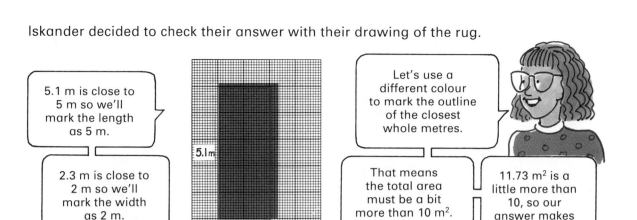

5.1 m is close to 5 m so we'll mark the length as 5 m.

2.3 m is close to 2 m so we'll mark the width as 2 m.

Let's use a different colour to mark the outline of the closest whole metres.

That means the total area must be a bit more than 10 m².

11.73 m² is a little more than 10, so our answer makes sense.

Iskander and Jenny worked out the approximate area of a different floor rug.

The closest whole numbers are *outside* our shape.

That means the total area must be a bit less than 6 m × 3 m.

Marking the closest whole metre is the same as rounding the number.

4 Find the exact area of the floor rug that measures 5.9 m by 2.8 m. Does this answer make sense?

5 Look at the rectangles you drew for Question 3. Follow Iskander and Jenny's steps to work out the approximate area. Were your exact answers reasonable?

6 Use the same steps to work out the approximate area of these rectangles. Calculate the exact area. Were your answers reasonable?

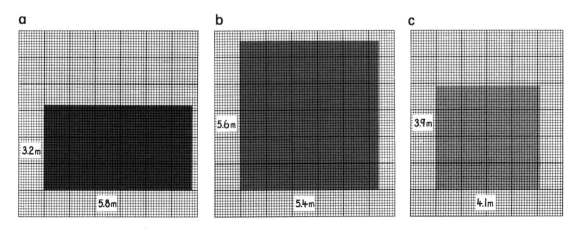

a 3.2 m, 5.8 m

b 5.6 m, 5.4 m

c 3.9 m, 4.1 m

Tom's class was doing a project on mass.
They wanted to find out about different types of weighing machines.
First they looked at machines that measured small amounts.

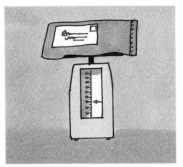  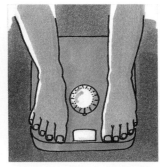

| These go up to 100 g | These go up to 4 kg | These go up to 126 kg |

The children went on an excursion to
Tom's dad's woodyard to look at scales
that measured large amounts. They
stacked the scales with 100 kg of firewood.

1 **Find the mass of a log.**

2 **About how many logs each
with an average mass of 3 kg
make up 100 kg?**

Tom's dad loaded his truck with one tonne of firewood.

| 1000 kilograms = one tonne | | One kilogram = one thousandth of a tonne |

3 **How many 100 kg loads in one tonne of firewood?**

4 **Do you think the total mass of the pupils in your class is greater or less than
one tonne? Check your answer.**

Joe and Helen decided to earn money during the holidays by making and selling lemonade. They made a flow diagram to help them plan for each day.

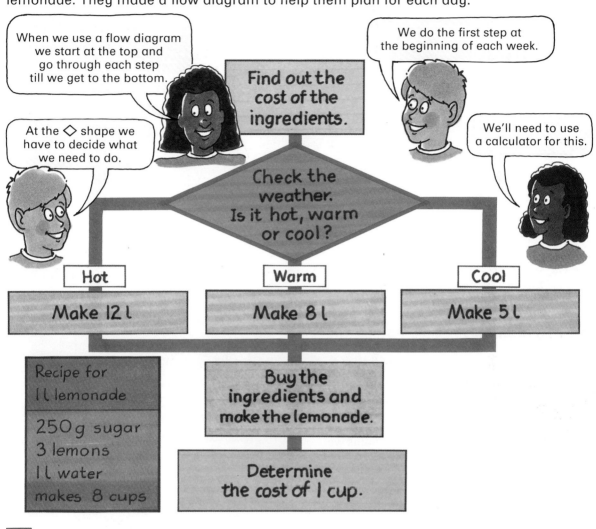

1 How much of each ingredient will they buy on a:

   a hot day   b warm day   c cool day?

2 Suppose that sugar costs 85p per kilogram, lemons cost 15p each, and paper cups are 95p per dozen.
   Estimate the total cost of ingredients on a:

   a hot day   b warm day   c cool day?

3 Work out to the nearest penny the cost of one cup of lemonade.

4 The children decided to make a profit of 9p per cup.
   What price should they charge per cup?

5 Since the profit per cup is 9p, how much profit will the children make on a:

   a hot day   b warm day   c cool day?

Lisa and Craig tried to find all the unit fractions they could write as hundredths.

> We know that we can write one-fifth as hundredths.

> That's because 5 is a factor of 100.

> We need to multiply 5 by 20 to get 100. We'll need to multiply the numerator by 20 as well.

$$\frac{1}{5} \overset{\times 20}{\underset{\times 20}{=}} \frac{\boxed{20}}{100}$$

1 **Copy these unit fractions.**

a $\frac{1}{4}$ b $\frac{1}{10}$ c $\frac{1}{20}$ d $\frac{1}{40}$ e $\frac{1}{50}$ f $\frac{1}{60}$ g $\frac{1}{75}$

● Loop the denominators that are factors of 100.

● Beneath each denominator you looped, write the number you would multiply it by to get 100.

2 **List all the unit fractions from $\frac{1}{2}$ to $\frac{1}{99}$.**

a Loop all the denominators that are factors of 100.

b How many unit fractions in your list can be written as hundredths?

> Here we have three-fifths.

> To write $\frac{3}{5}$ as hundredths we need to multiply both the denominator and the numerator by 20.

$$\frac{3}{5} \overset{\times 20}{\underset{\times 20}{=}} \frac{\boxed{60}}{100}$$

> So three-fifths is the same as 60 hundredths.

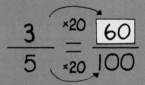

3 **Copy these fractions.**

a $\frac{2}{5} = \frac{\square}{100}$ b $\frac{7}{10} = \frac{\square}{100}$ c $\frac{8}{25} = \frac{\square}{100}$ d $\frac{19}{20} = \frac{\square}{100}$

● Draw the arrows, and write what you have to multiply the denominator by to get hundredths.

● Fill in the box to complete the equivalent fraction.

Decimal Dice Cover-up
For 2 to 10 players

● Use a wooden cube as a die.
● Write on the faces: 1 hundredth, 1 fiftieth, 1 twentieth,
                 1 tenth, 1 fifth, 1 quarter.
● Each player needs a hundredths grid and coloured pencils.

Rules
● Take turns to roll the die.
● Players colour the fraction of their grid that matches the fraction on the die.
● The first player to colour the whole grid wins.

Louise and Tom were showing their mother the fraction game they played at school.

> We have to match the word and symbol cards to each picture.

> This one has 45 of the hundredths coloured.

> Here are two decimal cards that match.

forty-five hundredths   0.45

Mrs Gordon said she knew another way.

> Do you know what the prefix *cent* means?

> Yes . . . we studied that last year.
>
> It comes from the word *centum*. That's Latin for hundred.

> You have coloured 45 out of one hundred parts.

> We can say we coloured 45 per hundred or 45 *per cent*.

These are the 2 new cards that Mrs Gordon made.
She called them *percentage* cards.

forty-five per cent

45%

> The symbol for per cent looks as if it has 2 zeros.

> A good way to think of it is as "out of one hundred".

1 Make your own set of 5 cards to show 45 per cent.

2 Make picture cards that match each of these.
Then make two decimal cards and two percentage cards for each.

a 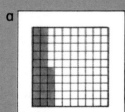 b 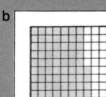 c 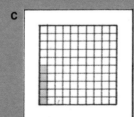 d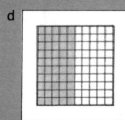

3 Make some more sets of cards for different percentages.
Use all the cards to play Rummy.

> Remember that one pound is the same as 100 pence

4 Some children saved these amounts
out of every pound they earned:

a Kim 50p   b Geoff 45p   c Nadia 10p   d Lee 75p   e Pearl 5p

● What fraction of each pound did each child save?
● What percentage did each child save?

Mrs Rust gave the children 10 cm by 10 cm squares to fold
to show different fractions.

Ella showed $\frac{1}{2}$ Paul showed $\frac{1}{4}$ Linda showed $\frac{3}{4}$

Mr Gold drew a grid that was the same size as each square.
He divided it into hundredths so that he could estimate what decimal
fraction was equivalent to each common fraction.

We can put
our grid
over each square.

We can count
about how many
hundredths take up
the same space.

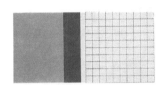

1 **Cut out three 10 cm x 10 cm squares.**

  ● Fold and colour them to show one-half,
    one-quarter and three-quarters.

  ● Use your grid to count how many hundredths take up the same space as each
    fraction you coloured.

  ● Estimate when you cannot count exactly.

  ● Write your estimate as a decimal fraction.

2 **Use what you already know to write the decimal fraction**
that is exactly equal to one-half, one-quarter and three-quarters.

3 **Fold and colour other 10 cm x 10 cm squares**
to show these fractions.

  a $\frac{1}{8}$ b $\frac{3}{8}$ c $\frac{5}{8}$ d $\frac{7}{8}$ e $\frac{1}{5}$ f $\frac{2}{5}$ g $\frac{3}{5}$ h $\frac{1}{3}$ i $\frac{2}{3}$

  ● Put the hundredths grid on top of each fraction and make an estimate of how
    many hundredths are equivalent to each fraction.
    Write your estimate as a decimal fraction.

Ruth and Barney wanted to find out which colour was the most popular for the whole school. First they took a survey of their own class. Then they made a graph of the results.

Questionnaire
Tick your favourite colour

☐ red   ☐ green   ☐ yellow
☐ blue   ☐ orange   ☐ purple

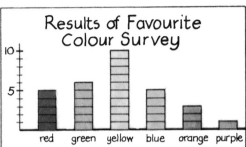

Results of Favourite Colour Survey

We could survey each child in the whole school, but that would be a lot of work.

Why don't we just do a survey of the children in our own class and then make a prediction based on that information?

1 How many children in the class answered the questionnaire?

2 Write as a fraction what part of the class chose each colour. Try to express each fraction in its lowest terms.

Now we can use the information from the *sample* of 30 children to make a prediction about the whole school.

About $\frac{1}{3}$ of the class chose yellow, so about $\frac{1}{3}$ of the school would do the same. To find $\frac{1}{3}$ of 252 we divide by 3.

$$\begin{array}{r} 84 \\ 3\overline{)252} \\ 24 \\ \hline 12 \\ 12 \\ \hline \end{array}$$

There are 252 children in the whole school and we'd expect about the same fraction to choose each colour.

That means we'd expect about 80 children in the school to say that yellow is their favourite colour.

3 Predict the number of children in Ruth and Barney's school who would pick as their favourite colour:

a red   b green   c blue   d orange   e purple.

4 Here are the results of a pet survey.

a How many children are in the sample?

b What fraction of the sample chose each pet?

c Predict how many children in Ruth and Barney's school would choose each pet.

Results of Favourite Pet Survey

8 dog   4 cat
3 horse   6 fish
3 bird   0 hamster

5 Conduct your own school 'favourite colour' and 'favourite pet' surveys. You could add some extra questions. Use your class as a sample and predict the results for the whole school.

Tim and Eileen were using fraction pies to show addition and subtraction.

It's easy to add and subtract fractions when they have the same bottom number.

$\frac{3}{8} + \frac{2}{8} = \boxed{}$ $\frac{5}{6} - \frac{1}{6} = \boxed{}$

The bottom number is called the denominator.

1 Write the answer for each of these.
You can use fraction shapes* to help.

a $\frac{1}{5} + \frac{3}{5} = \boxed{}$ b $\frac{2}{7} + \frac{4}{7} = \boxed{}$ c $\frac{3}{4} + \frac{1}{4} = \boxed{}$ d $\frac{1}{3} + \frac{2}{3} = \boxed{}$

e $\frac{7}{8} - \frac{3}{8} = \boxed{}$ f $\frac{11}{12} - \frac{7}{12} = \boxed{}$ g $\frac{15}{16} - \frac{11}{16} = \boxed{}$ h $\frac{4}{4} - \frac{3}{4} = \boxed{}$

How can we add these? The bottom numbers are different . . . but they're closely related.

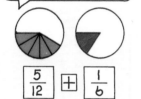

$\frac{5}{12}$ ⊞ $\frac{1}{6}$

I'll swap $\frac{1}{6}$ for $\frac{2}{12}$.

We can easily change sixths to twelfths . . . 12 is a multiple of 6.

We only need to change one of the numbers to get the bottom numbers the same.

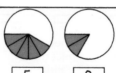

$\frac{5}{12}$ ⊞ $\frac{2}{12}$

It's easy to add or subtract when the fractions have the same denominator.

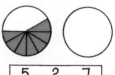

$\frac{5}{12} + \frac{2}{12} = \frac{7}{12}$

2 Use fraction shapes to help you add these.

a

$\frac{1}{4}$ ⊞ $\frac{5}{8}$

b

$\frac{7}{9}$ ⊞ $\frac{2}{3}$

c

$\frac{1}{3}$ ⊞ $\frac{5}{12}$

3 Use fraction shapes to help you subtract these.

a

$\frac{5}{6}$ ⊟ $\frac{1}{12}$

b

$\frac{3}{4}$ ⊟ $\frac{5}{12}$

c

$\frac{1}{3}$ ⊟ $\frac{4}{15}$

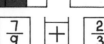

* Templates included on *Duplicate Masters 45, 46, 47, 48.*

Mr Sinclair's class made a special study of three-dimensional shapes in the world around them. They found and made a collection of solids to sort in many different ways. Some children read that solids with no curved surfaces belong to the *polyhedron* family.

> Shapes with all flat surfaces can be called *polyhedra*.

> In Greek, *hedra* is the plural form of *hedron*.

1 | **Talk about the solids in the picture below.**

a Point to the shapes which have all surfaces flat.

b Make or find some polyhedra.

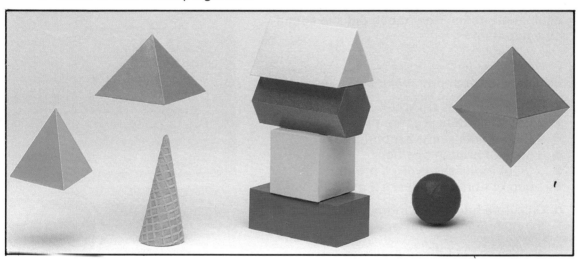

Euler, a Swiss mathematician, noticed a pattern when he counted the faces, edges and vertices of polyhedra.

> Euler is pronounced 'oiler'. He lived from 1707 to 1783.

2 | **Use real solids to match the frameworks in this chart.**

a Copy and complete the table. (Add more if you can.)

b Look for a pattern in the last two columns.

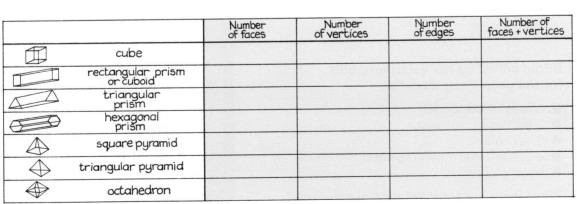

		Number of faces	Number of vertices	Number of edges	Number of faces + vertices
	cube				
	rectangular prism or cuboid				
	triangular prism				
	hexagonal prism				
	square pyramid				
	triangular pyramid				
	octahedron				

Brigid was given a horse by her parents. After one year, they asked Brigid to work out the expenses. Brigid collected this information to help.

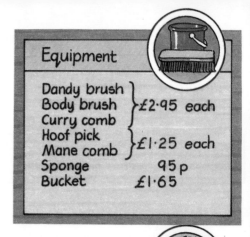

Equipment

Dandy brush	}£2·95 each
Body brush	
Curry comb	
Hoof pick	}£1·25 each
Mane comb	
Sponge	95p
Bucket	£1·65

1 Throughout the year, Brigid bought 3 buckets, 2 curry combs and 1 each of the other equipment items. How much did she spend on equipment?

Feed

Bale of hay	£ 2·85
Bag of chaff	£ 8·75
Bag of oats	£11·50
Bag of bran	£10·95
Large tin of molasses	£ 7·95
Bag of horse mix	£12·35

2 Brigid estimated that Jacko ate:

● a bale of hay every week
● a bag of chaff every month
● a bag of oats every 2 months
● 3 bags of bran in one year
● a tin of molasses every 4 months
● 1 bag of horse mix every 3 months.

  a Calculate how much money was spent for each feed item for one year.

  b What was the total feed bill for one year?

Basic Needs

Bridle	£28·00
Shoeing (every 6 weeks)	£25·00
Blankets	£19·00
Livery (weekly)	£ 9·50
Registration (yearly)	£23·00

3 Kate's horse was in livery for 6 months. In that time there were no feed bills.

  a What was the cost of the livery for 6 months?

  b How does this compare with the cost of feed for 6 months?

  c What would be the total cost for feeding Jacko for one year if he was in livery for 6 months?

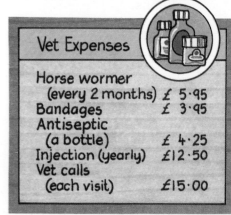

Vet Expenses

Horse wormer (every 2 months)	£ 5·95
Bandages	£ 3·95
Antiseptic (a bottle)	£ 4·25
Injection (yearly)	£12·50
Vet calls (each visit)	£15·00

4 Brigid added up her veterinary bills for the year. They were for:

● 6 rolls of bandages
● 3 bottles of antiseptic
● 5 vet calls
● wormer (every two months)
● yearly injection.

What were her total veterinary expenses?

Brigid wanted to take her horse to shows. Her parents asked her to work out some of the costs first.

1 Brigid's parents said they would buy the showing jacket if Brigid would pay for all the other gear out of her allowance.

    a How much more does the jacket cost than the rest of the riding gear?

    b Brigid will pay £3 from her allowance each week to pay for the rest of the riding gear. Can she pay for it in one year?

2 Brigid estimates she will need one riding lesson a fortnight for 6 months. How much will this cost?

3 The directions on the bottle of shampoo say to use $\frac{1}{4}$ of the bottle each time. If the horse is shampooed every week, what is the cost for shampoo in one year?

4 There are 7 horse shows each year. It is necessary to travel, on average, 85 km for the round trip for each show. Calculate these costs for the year.

    a Horse-box hire.

    b Car travel costs.

    c Entry fees for Brigid, her parents, her brother and one guest each time.

    d The total cost for horse-box hire, car travel and entry fees for all 7 horse shows.

5 One horse box boot was lost. Is £5·50 a fair replacement cost for one boot?

Riding Gear

Approved riding helmet	£ 38·50
Velvet cap	£ 19·75
Riding boots	£ 47·50
Jodhpurs	£ 37·95
Showing jacket	£150·00

Accessories

Riding lessons (per hour)	£ 7·50
Oilskin coat	£89·00
Hoof block (per tin)	£ 2·50
Shampoo (per bottle)	£ 2·95

Travel Expenses

Horse-box hire (daily)	£18·75
Horse-box boots (set of 4)	£21·80
Car Travel (per kilometre)	35p

Club Fees

Entry (each show)	
members	£1·50
members family	80p
others	£2·50
Entry (each event)	50p

Mr Boyd's class decided to sell peaches at the fête to raise money.
They sent Sophie and Daniel to the market to find out prices.

1 Calculate the unit price for peaches in:

   a the box of 50 peaches   b the box of 80 peaches.

2 Which box has the lower unit price?

Which size box would you choose?

3 Calculate the unit price for peaches in all the other boxes.

4 Which box of peaches has:

   a the cheapest unit price   b the dearest unit price?

5 Calculate the cost of 10 peaches in:

   a the box of 50 peaches   b the box of 80 peaches.

6 Which box has the lower cost for 10 peaches?

7 Calculate the cost of buying 10 peaches from each of the other boxes.

8 Which box of peaches has:

   a the cheapest price for 10 peaches   b the dearest price for 10 peaches?

1. What is the price of 4 boxes of 20 peaches? Which is the better buy?

2. Use the same steps to decide which is the better buy each time.

a
| 20 oranges for £4·98 |
| or |
| 60 oranges for £13·99 |

b
| 10 pears for £2·79 |
| or |
| 40 pears for £9·99 |

c
| 30 apples for £7·85 |
| or |
| 60 apples for £15·50 |

3. Look at the picture of the peaches on page 70. What other pairs of boxes could you compare in the same way?

4. Compare the prices of each pair by multiplying the price of the smaller box. Write which box is the better buy in each pair.

5. Identify those pairs of amounts of cheese you can compare quickly in the picture below. Then multiply the price of the smaller amount in each pair to see which is the better buy.

6. A recipe calls for 350 g of cheese.
List the different ways you could buy this amount.
Work out the price for each way.

Sally and Melvin were checking the prices in a Christmas catalogue.

1 Calculate how much money Sally and Melvin should save each week for 5 months if they want to buy these items:

a radio   b tennis racquet   c typewriter   d bicycle.

2 Suppose Sally and Melvin started to save money 6 months before Christmas. Calculate how much they would need to save each week to buy the:

a radio   b tennis racquet   c typewriter   d bicycle   e CD player.

3 Suppose the children started to save eight months before Christmas. Calculate how much they would need to save each week to buy each item in Question 2.

4 What is the difference between the amount saved each week for a 6-month period and for an 8-month period?

At school, Sally and Melvin checked their calculations with their teacher.

our method works,

but you could have divided by 20.

5×4 weeks = 20 weeks

$$4.45$$
$$20\overline{)89.00}$$
$$80$$
$$9\,0$$
$$8\,0$$
$$\overline{1\,00}$$

This is just an estimate.

$$22\overline{)89.00}$$

There are 22 weeks in 5 months.

If you divide by 22 you'll get a closer answer.

When you divide by a 2-digit number ask the same questions hat you used or dividing by a 1-digit number.

There won't be any tens in the answer, but we can get ones.

$$4.$$
$$22\overline{)89.00}$$
$$88$$
$$\overline{1\,0}$$

This means that you must still save at least £4 each week.

But it is not as much as £4·45.

4.0455

A calculator will give you a more exact answer.

---

1 Calculate how much money Sally and Melvin need to save each week for 20 weeks to buy the:

   a radio   **b** tennis racquet   **c** typewriter   **d** bicycle.

2 Imagine Melvin and Sally decided to save for 22 weeks. About how much money do you think they'll need to save each week?

3 Use a calculator to get the exact results in Question 2.

4 Calculate how much money Sally and Melvin would need to save each week for 30 weeks to buy the:

   a CD player   **b** radio   **c** tennis racquet   **d** typewriter   **e** bicycle.

5 The calculator displays show the exact amount they would need to save for 32 weeks to buy the same items. Use your results from Question 4 to tell which ones do not seem right.

   a CD player   **b** radio   **c** tennis racquet   **d** typewriter   **e** bicycle

   | 2.75 | 1.05 | 2.25 | 2.30 | 4.00 |

6 Write an estimate of how much Sally and Melvin should save each week for 40 weeks to buy each item. Then check your estimates.

Yasmin showed her young brother Jamil the diagram of an experiment she did at secondary school.

1 **Discuss Yasmin's diagram.**

2 **Copy and complete these statements.**

  a . . . . millilitres = 1 litre.

  b one millilitre has the same volume as . . . . cubic centimetre.

  c . . . . cm³ of sand will fill a 100 ml container.

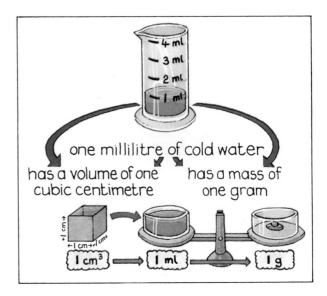

one millilitre of cold water

has a volume of one cubic centimetre   has a mass of one gram

1 cm³ ⟶ 1 ml ⟶ 1 g

Jamil's group did some experiments with larger metric units.

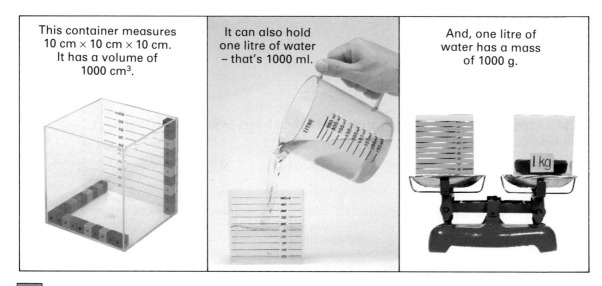

This container measures 10 cm × 10 cm × 10 cm. It has a volume of 1000 cm³.

It can also hold one litre of water – that's 1000 ml.

And, one litre of water has a mass of 1000 g.

3 **Carry out your own experiments with a one-litre container of water.**

  a Record the volume of the water:
    ● in cubic centimetres   ● in millilitres.

  b Discuss the best way to find the net mass of water when it is weighed in a container.

  c Record the net mass of one litre of cold water:
    ● in grams   ● in kilograms.

4 **Copy and complete this table.**

Volume in litres	Volume in ml	Volume in cm³
2 l		
3 l		
5 l		
10 l		

Kay's group did some different experiments with volume.
They made a small brick of centicubes.

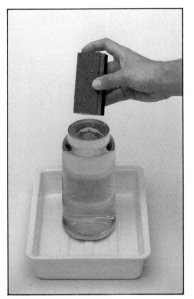

The brick measures
10 cm × 5 cm × 3 cm.
It has a volume of 150 cm³.

To find how much water
it displaces, measure
the overflow.

150 ml

The brick displaced
150 ml of water.

1 **Use the pictures of Kay's experiment to help you decide how many millilitres of water would take up the same amount of space as a brick with a volume of:**

a 250 cm³   **b** 100 cm³   **c** 1000 cm³   **d** 1 cm³.

One millilitre has the same volume
as one cubic centimetre.

The volume of something
tells how much space
it occupies.

Volume is measured
in cubic units like
cm³ or m³ . . .
but liquid volume
is often measured in
units related to the litre.

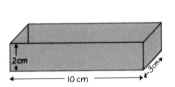
2cm   10 cm   3cm

3cm   7cm   2cm

5cm   3cm   3cm

2 **These drawings above show the dimensions of some containers.**

a Copy and continue the table below.

b Underline the largest volume in red.

c Discuss your results.

I can hold 60 cm³
of material.
That's my capacity.

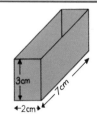

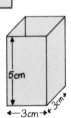

I'll call that 60 ml
if the material is liquid.

Inside dimensions			Volume in cm³	Number of cm³ blocks to fill box	Capacity in millilitres
length	width	height			
3 cm	3 cm	5 cm	. . . . . .	. . . .	. . . . . .
10 cm	3 cm	2 cm	. . . . . .	. . . .	. . . . . .

The 5 children were given 4 toffee bars to share.

 How can we do the sharing fairly?

 We can divide each bar into fifths.

Then each of us would get 4 of the fifths.

1 Share the toffee bars in each picture among 5 children. Write the amount each child will get as a common fraction.

a 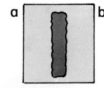 b   c

 We know another way to share. $5\overline{)4}$

We can divide the 4 bars among five children.

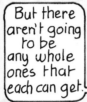 But there aren't going to be any whole ones that each can get.

$$\begin{array}{r} 0.8 \\ 5\overline{)4.0} \\ 4\ 0 \\ \hline 0 \end{array}$$

We'll need to swap each one for tenths.

 That's 8 tenths for each.

We already know that $\frac{4}{5}$ and 0.8 are the same.

2 Now divide the number of bars shown in each toffee-bar picture among 5 children. But this time:

a write the amount each child will get as a decimal fraction

b check that the decimal-fraction answers are equivalent to the common-fraction answers you wrote for Question 1.

> When we want to find a decimal fraction that is equivalent to a common fraction, we can do it quickly by dividing the numerator by the denominator.

Four children were given 3 cakes to share.

 We know that is $\frac{3}{4}$ of a cake for each.

If we divide 3 by 4 we can write each share as a decimal.
$$\begin{array}{r} 0.7 \\ 4\overline{)3.0} \\ 2\ 8 \\ \hline 2 \end{array}$$

There are still 2 tenths left so we'll need to swap for hundredths.
$$\begin{array}{r} 0.75 \\ 4\overline{)3.00} \\ 2\ 8 \\ \hline 2\ 0 \\ 2\ 0 \\ \hline 0 \end{array}$$

That's 75 hundredths as a decimal.

3 Share the cakes in each of these pictures among 4 children.

a Write the amount that each gets as a common fraction.

b Find out how much each gets when the amount is written as a decimal fraction.

a

b

David and Gwen collected cans for five days.
They made a graph to show the number they collected each day.

The children listed the numbers they collected in order from greatest to least.

1 **What was the greatest number of cans collected in one day?**

2 **What was the least number of cans collected in one day?**

3 **How many numbers are on the list?**

4 **Which number is in the exact middle of the range?**

The number that occurs in the exact middle of a list of numbers written in order from greatest to least is called the *median*.

5 **The children collected cans for another four weeks.**
For each week:

a list the numbers in order from greatest to least

b write the number that is the median

c calculate the range.

	Mon	Tue	Wed	Thu	Fri	Median
Week 1	25	10	10	15	15	
Week 2	6	0	19	21	21	
Week 3	16	17	18	19	20	
Week 4	18	14	18	24	23	

Mrs Taylor's class marked out these rectangles in the playground.
They made the dimensions different, but made sure their measurements included the same digits each time.

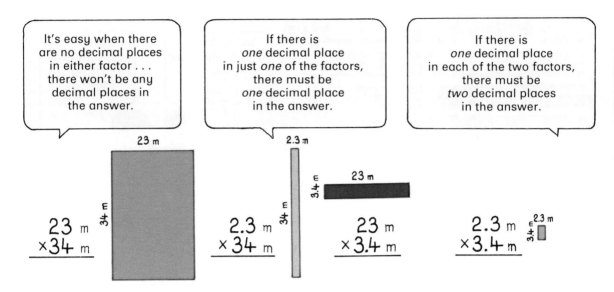

It's easy when there are no decimal places in either factor . . . there won't be any decimal places in the answer.

If there is *one* decimal place in just *one* of the factors, there must be *one* decimal place in the answer.

If there is *one* decimal place in each of the two factors, there must be *two* decimal places in the answer.

23 m
×34 m

2.3 m
×34 m

23 m
×3.4 m

2.3 m
×3.4 m

1 Calculate the area of each rectangle. Place the decimal point when you have finished each calculation.

2 This table gives the dimensions of many rectangles. Calculate the area of each rectangle, then copy the table and fill in the answers.

a In each column, what do you notice about the digits in the answers?

b In each row, what is the total number of decimal places in the dimensions?

c In each row, how many decimal places are there in each answer?

d What do you notice about the answers in the second and third rows?

a 32 m × 31 m ..... m²	b 28 m × 29 m ..... m²	c 37 m × 23 m ..... m²	d 26 m × 34 m ..... m²	e 38 m × 25 m ..... m²
3.2 m × 31 m ..... m²	2.8 m × 29 m ..... m²	3.7 m × 23 m ..... m²	2.6 m × 34 m ..... m²	3.8 m × 25 m ..... m²
32 m × 3.1 m ..... m²	28 m × 2.9 m ..... m²	37 m × 2.3 m ..... m²	26 m × 3.4 m ..... m²	38 m × 2.5 m ..... m²
3.2 m × 3.1 m ..... m²	2.8 m × 2.9 m ..... m²	3.7 m × 2.3 m ..... m²	2.6 m × 3.4 m ..... m²	3.8 m × 2.5 m ..... m²

3 Check to make sure that your answers in Question 2 make sense.

● Round each dimension in the table to the nearest ten (for whole numbers), or nearest one (for decimals).

● Use these rounded numbers to make another table.

● Multiply the rounded numbers. Compare your approximate answers with your exact answers. Are your exact answers reasonable?

Jane and Adam marked out two more rectangles.
They made the dimensions different but used measurements with the
same digits each time.

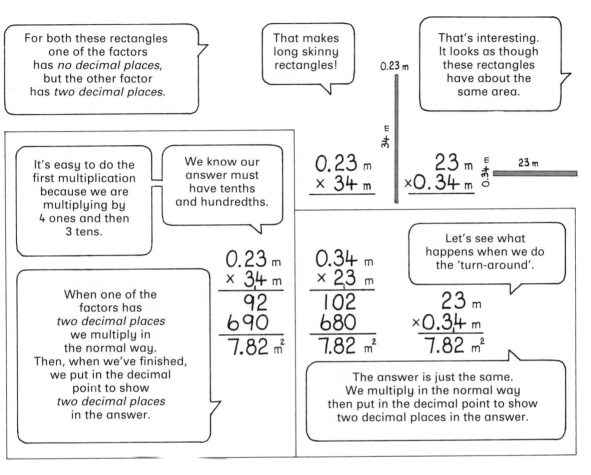

For both these rectangles
one of the factors
has *no decimal places*,
but the other factor
has *two decimal places*.

That makes
long skinny
rectangles!

That's interesting.
It looks as though
these rectangles
have about the
same area.

It's easy to do the
first multiplication
because we are
multiplying by
4 ones and then
3 tens.

We know our
answer must
have tenths
and hundredths.

When one of the
factors has
two decimal places
we multiply in
the normal way.
Then, when we've finished,
we put in the decimal
point to show
two decimal places
in the answer.

Let's see what
happens when we do
the 'turn-around'.

The answer is just the same.
We multiply in the normal way
then put in the decimal point to show
two decimal places in the answer.

0.23 m
× 34 m
─────
  92
 690
─────
7.82 m²

0.34 m
× 23 m
─────
 102
 680
─────
7.82 m²

  23 m
×0.34 m
─────
7.82 m²

4   Look at your answers to Question 1. Can you find a rectangle that
has the same area as each of Jane and Adam's two rectangles?

5   Copy this table and fill
in the answers. Use
short cuts if you can.

6   Do you notice any
patterns in this table?
Are the patterns the
same as in the table on page 78?

a 0.32 m	b 0.28 m	c 0.37 m	d 0.26 m	e 0.38 m
× 31 m	× 29 m	× 23 m	× 34 m	× 25 m
..... m²	..... m²	..... m²	..... m²	..... m²
32 m	28 m	37 m	26 m	38 m
× 0.31 m	× 0.29 m	× 0.23 m	× 0.34 m	× 0.25 m
..... m²	..... m²	..... m²	..... m²	..... m²

When you multiply numbers with decimals, it's easier to
put in the decimal point when you have completed the calculation.
The number of decimal places in the answer will be the same
as the sum of the number of decimal places in the factors.

This cricket bag is very heavy. What do you think the total mass might be?

Let's measure to find out. Our scales only go up to 5 kg so we'll have to find the mass of each item. Then we'll add to find the total.

The children wrote the mass of each item in kilograms.

MASS OF CRICKET GEAR

bat	1.1 kg	2 batting gloves	0.15 kg each	2 bails	0.05 kg each
bat	0.9 kg	2 keeper's gloves	0.375 kg each	6 stumps	0.4 kg each
		2 shoes	0.4 kg each		
ball	0.156 kg	2 leg pads	0.9 kg each	helmet	0.455 kg
bag	2.65 kg	Cricket jumper	0.45 kg	3 oranges	0.15 kg each
Sun hat	0.06 kg	Sunblock cream	0.3 kg	1 can of drink	0.5 kg

We need to be careful when we add and subtract numbers with decimals.

```
  1.1   kg
-0.455 kg
```

```
  1.100 kg
-0.455 kg
```

Yes, we have to make sure each 'place' lines up. Sometimes it helps to put in zeros to hold the places.

1 Calculate the difference in mass for each pair of items.

a the bag and 2 keeper's gloves

b the ball and the large bat

c 1 orange and 1 can of drink

d 2 batting gloves and 2 keeper's gloves

2 Find the total mass for each list of items.

a
Large bat
Ball
Helmet
2 leg pads

b
2 keeper's gloves
2 leg pads
6 stumps
2 bails

c
2 shoes
Jumper
2 leg pads
2 batting gloves

d
2 oranges
Can of drink
Sun hat
Sun cream

3 What is the mass of all the items, including the bag?

4 Make up bags of gear for some other sports.

a Find the mass of each item.

b Compare the mass of the heaviest and lightest item in each bag.

c Find the total mass of all the items in each bag.

Mandy and Clive tried to find the mass of one pencil.

It's too hard to measure one pencil accurately with our scales.

Why not put several pencils all the same on the scales? Say 30 pencils.

Then we can divide the total mass by the number of pencils.

Let's divide to get thousandths. Then we can round to the nearest hundredth of a gram.

Step 1   **Step 2**   **Step 3**

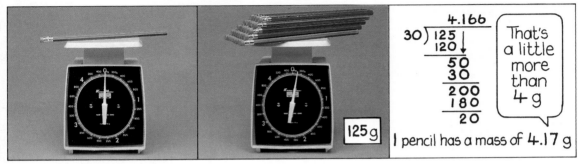

$$30\overline{)125}$$

4.166

That's a little more than 4 g

125 g

I pencil has a mass of 4.17 g

---

1 Weigh some pencils yourself. Use the steps above to find the approximate mass of one pencil for each of these collections of pencils. Take your answers to the nearest hundredth of a gram. (You can use a calculator.)

    a 10 pencils   **b** 20 pencils   **c** 30 pencils   **d** 25 pencils

2 Were your answers in Question 1 about the same each time?

3 Calculate the mass of one item in each of these collections.

  a   **b**   **c**   **d**

| 20 erasers had a total mass of 275 g | 50 paper clips had a mass of 28 g | 40 small nails had a mass of 85 g | 30 large nails had a mass of 185 g |

4 Find the total mass of some other collections of small objects: erasers; paper clips; 5p coins; small nails; large nails.
Use the total mass to work out the approximate mass of one item in each collection.

5 Here are some division answers. Work out what each dividend would have been if you had divided by 20 to get the answer. Then write what the dividends would have been if you had divided by 30.

  a   **b**   **c**   **d**   **e**   **f**

  26.5   2.65   0.265   9   0.9   0.09

Ricky and Rita tried to work out how many toothpicks they would need for the next shape in each pattern.

Pattern 1			Pattern 2			Pattern 3		
	Number of squares	Number of toothpicks		Number of squares	Number of toothpicks		Number of squares	Number of toothpicks
	1	4		1	4		1	4
	2	7		3	10		5	16
	3	10		5	16		9	28
	____	____		____	____		____	____
	____	____		____	____		____	____

1 **For each pattern:**

   a Write the missing information for the fourth and fifth pictures.

   b Draw the next shape in the sequence.

   c Count the number of squares and the number of toothpicks in the pictures you drew.

Now Ricky and Rita made a growing square of squares.

Total number of squares	1	5	14	____	____
Total number of toothpicks	4	12	24	____	____

2 **For the 'Square of Squares' pattern:**

   a Write the missing information for the fourth and fifth pictures.

   b Draw the next 3 pictures in the sequence.

   c Count the number of squares and the number of toothpicks in the pictures you drew.

3 Work out the total number of squares in a 10 by 10 square of squares.

The children at Mill Hill School decided
to have a table tennis tournament.
They needed to work out a draw for 120 children.

How many
games will we need
to play altogether?

Let's try to
calculate.

RULES
• Everyone plays.
• When you lose once,
  you are out of the
  tournament.

The children discussed how they could work out the total number of games to be
played. They said they could:
● act out the tournament   ● draw a diagram   ● try to calculate.

1 **Discuss how you could solve the problem with each of these methods.**

That's pretty hard
with 120.

Why not try
it with a
smaller number?

What number
shall we pick?

The smaller the number the
quicker we can do it.
Let's try 2 or 3.

2 **Copy this chart and fill in the number of games that would be played.**
    Try to find a pattern.

Number of players	2	3	4	5	6	7	8	9	10
Number of games									

3 **How many games will be played by 120 children?**

When we
replace a large
number with a
smaller number
we are
simplifying the
story.

When the number in a story is large, replace it with a
smaller number. Try to work out the answer for
several smaller numbers. Then hunt for a pattern.

The class was picking 3 monitors out of 28 children.
They wanted to know how many different ways they could do it.
They looked for a pattern with several smaller numbers.

4 **Copy this chart and fill in the number of different ways for each number**
    of children.

Number of children	3	4	5	6	7	8	9	10	15	20	25	28
Number of different ways												

Josie and Tim drew patterns on dot paper to help work out what instructions to give the turtle on the computer.

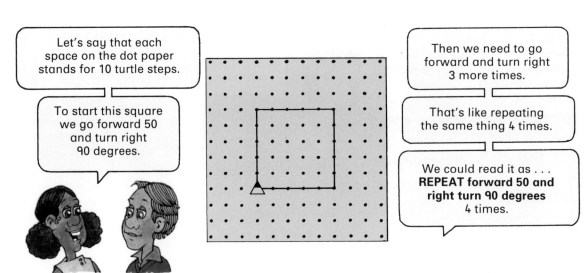

Let's say that each space on the dot paper stands for 10 turtle steps.

To start this square we go forward 50 and turn right 90 degrees.

Then we need to go forward and turn right 3 more times.

That's like repeating the same thing 4 times.

We could read it as . . .
REPEAT forward 50 and right turn 90 degrees 4 times.

Here are some more shapes Josie and Tim drew.

1 **Write the instructions to draw each shape without using REPEAT.**

The turtle tells you where to start and finish. Make sure you get it back to exactly the same place where it started.

2 **Now rewrite your instructions a quicker way using REPEAT.**

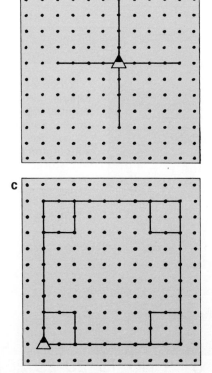

a

c

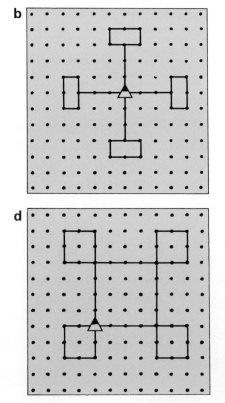

b

d

3 **Work out a different way to draw each shape.**

Billy is in the fourth year and he still forgets to put a decimal point in some of his figures.

14·95 cm?
149.5 cm?
14.95 cm?
1.4·95 cm?

1 **Add decimal points to these figures so that Billy's measurements will be reasonable when you copy his sentences.**

a I am 115 years old.

b My height is 1495 centimetres.

c I walk 225 kilometres to school each day.

d My foot length is 25 metres.

e My body mass is 352 kilograms.

f I heat the milk for my cereal in a 75-litre saucepan.

g The area of our class-room is 6475 square metres.

Betty is very good at measuring but she sometimes forgets to record the unit she used.

2 **Copy these sentences and complete them by choosing the unit you expect Betty should have used to record each of these measurements.**

a Our family car has a mass of about one ....

b The sports area in our playground is about one ....

c The circumference of our dustbin is about one ....

d Our telephone has a mass of about one ....

e The drawing pin has a mass of about one ....

f The ice-cream container has a capacity of about two ....

g The area of my bed is about two ....

h The volume of air in the telephone box is about two ....

i The perimeter of our doormat is about two ....

j A one-penny coin has a mass of about two ....

k Our telephone book has a mass of about two ....

3 **Copy this measurement table in a booklet. Find an example for each of these units. Make them different from those on this page.**

10 mm = 1 cm	1000 ml = 1 litre	1000 g = 1 kg
1000 mm = 1 m	1000 l = 1 kl	1000 kg = 1 tonne
100 cm = 1 m	1 cm³ = 1 ml	
1000 m = 1 km	1 m³ = 1000 litres	

Estimate before you measure.

Just find a picture for the very large units.

Becky and Joseph used a fraction wall to find common denominators so that they could add and subtract fractions.

How can we rename thirds and fifths so that they have a common denominator?

We'll need to find a common multiple of 3 and 5.

one whole
2 halves
3 thirds
4 quarters
5 fifths
6 sixths
7 sevenths
8 eighths
9 ninths
10 tenths
11 elevenths
12 twelfths
13 thirteenths
14 fourteenths
15 fifteenths
16 sixteenths

Becky and Joseph stretched a piece of string down the fraction wall to help find the multiple that is common to both 3 and 5. This showed them a common denominator of thirds and fifths.

1 **Look at the fraction wall. Use it to help you.**

   a List all the members of the thirds family.

   b Write all the members of the fifths family.

   c Did you find a member that was common to both?

Becky and Joseph wanted to add $\frac{2}{3}$ and $\frac{1}{5}$.

They recorded these equivalent fractions so that they could find a denominator common to both families.

Names for $\frac{2}{3}$: $\frac{2}{3}, \frac{4}{6}, \frac{6}{9}, \frac{8}{12}, \frac{10}{15}, \ldots$

Names for $\frac{1}{5}$: $\frac{1}{5}, \frac{2}{10}, \frac{3}{15}, \ldots$

2 **What is special about the denominators they coloured red?**

When Becky and Joseph had found a common denominator, they were able to find equivalent fractions and then add.

$$\frac{2}{3} + \frac{1}{5} =$$
$$\frac{10}{15} + \frac{3}{15} = \frac{13}{15}$$

The total is 13 fifteenths.

3 **Find the lowest common denominator for each pair of fractions in these examples. Work out equivalent fractions, then add or subtract.**

   a $\frac{1}{3} + \frac{1}{4} =$

   b $\frac{1}{2} + \frac{3}{7} =$

   c $\frac{3}{4} + \frac{1}{12} =$

   d $\frac{6}{6} + \frac{1}{4} =$

   e $\frac{1}{3} - \frac{1}{4} =$

   f $\frac{1}{2} - \frac{1}{7} =$

   g $\frac{3}{5} - \frac{1}{2} =$

   h $\frac{1}{3} - \frac{1}{6} =$

Chris and Cindy are trying to find the decimal fraction that is exactly the same as $\frac{1}{8}$.

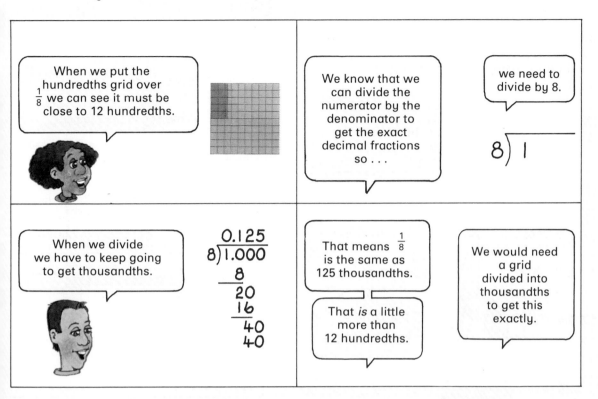

1 Write the decimal fraction that is the same as:

   a $\frac{3}{8}$ b $\frac{5}{8}$ c $\frac{7}{8}$ d $\frac{2}{8}$ e $\frac{4}{8}$ f $\frac{6}{8}$.

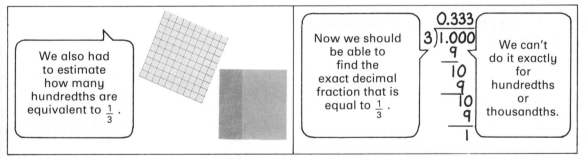

2 About how many hundredths equal $\frac{1}{3}$?

3 About how many thousandths equal $\frac{1}{3}$?

4 Use your calculator to find the decimal equivalent of $\frac{1}{3}$.

5 For each of these common fractions, find the equivalent decimal fraction, to the closest thousandth.

   a $\frac{2}{3}$ b $\frac{1}{6}$ c $\frac{5}{6}$ d $\frac{7}{20}$ e $\frac{15}{20}$ f $\frac{6}{25}$.

Mrs Moore's class collected information from 100 children in the first, second and third years. They tabulated the information for each question. For the first question they counted the number of letters in each name. They put the results in a table.

Questionnaire

1. What is your first name?

....

2. How many pets do you have at home?

....

3. How many children in your family?

....

1 Construct a graph of the results in the table opposite.

There are 8 names with 3 letters.

That's 8 out of 100 or 8 hundredths of the total. We write this as 0.08.

When we know the decimal fraction it is easy to find the percentage.

That means that 8 per cent of the total had 3 letters. We write this as 8%.

Counting letters in first names				
3	letters		8	
4	letters		15	
5	letters		21	
6	letters		24	
7	letters		7	
8	letters		18	
9	letters		6	
10	letters		0	
11	letters		1	

2 Write the decimal fraction that tells what part of the total number of names had 4, 5, 6, 7, 8, 9, 10 or 11 letters.

3 Write the percentage that tells what part of the total had names with 4, 5, 6, 7, 8, 9, 10 or 11 letters.

A class in the 4th year also answered the questionnaire. Here are the results they got.

Counting letters in first names				
4	letters		4	
5	letters		5	
6	letters		7	
7	letters		1	
8	letters		6	
9	letters		2	

4 How many children answered the questionnaire?

5 Write the decimal fraction that tells what part of the total had names with 4, 5, 6, 7, 8 or 9 letters.
You may use a calculator to do this.

You can write a common fraction first. Then divide to get the decimal fraction of the same value.

6 Write your answers to Question 5 as percentages.

7 Conduct your own survey. Tabulate the results for each question. Then calculate the percentage of children who got each result.

Mr Green's class measured their class-room so that they could make a plan of it. They decided to let every *5 millimetres* on the paper stand for *one metre* on the ground. This was the scale of their plan.

Scale : 5 mm stands for 1 m
0m 1 2 3 4 5 6 7 8 9 10

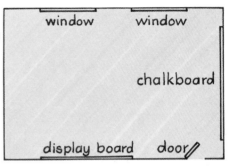

window   window

chalkboard

display board   door

1 **Use the scale to find the real measurements for these:**

    a length of room   **b** width of room   **c** width of each window

    d width of door   **e** length of display board   **f** length of chalkboard.

2 **Measure your own class-room and draw plans at these two scales.**

    ● **1 cm stands for 1 metre**   ● **5 cm stands for one metre**

    Which plan would be suitable for an exercise book? . . . a wall chart?

Hanna brought to school this map of a bus route.

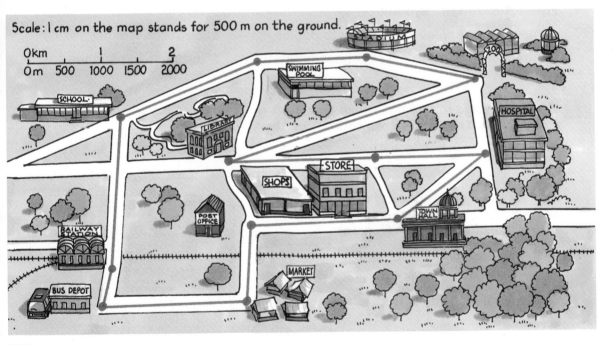

Scale : 1 cm on the map stands for 500 m on the ground.

0km   1   2
0m   500   1000   1500   2000

SCHOOL ·   SWIMMING POOL   STADIUM   ZOO   HOSPITAL   LIBRARY   STORE   SHOPS   POST OFFICE   TOWN HALL   RAILWAY STATION   MARKET   BUS DEPOT

3 **Measure on the map, then use the scale to help you work out the real distances for these bus routes.**

    a school to pool   **b** pool to stadium   **c** stadium to zoo

    d zoo to library   **e** library to hospital   **f** post office to bus depot

4 **Use the scale on Hanna's map and continue the table up to 10 centimetres.**

On the map	On the ground
1 cm	500 m
2 cm	1000 m (1 km)
3 cm	1500 m (1.5 km)

89

Glenn and Celia used this recipe to make fruit salad for dessert. Their older sister told them they could use *ratio* to compare the amount of one ingredient with another.

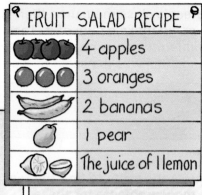

FRUIT SALAD RECIPE

🍎🍎🍎	4 apples
🍊🍊🍊	3 oranges
🍌🍌	2 bananas
🍐	1 pear
🍋	The juice of 1 lemon

The recipe says to put in 4 apples and 3 oranges.

Right.... that's 4 apples to 3 oranges.

We can say that the ratio of apples to oranges is 4 to 3.

4 to 3

Here's a simple way to write the ratio.

4 : 3

1 Compare the quantities of each two fruits as they are used in the recipe. Write each ratio with the symbol.

    a bananas to apples   **b** pears to apples   **c** pears to oranges

    d bananas to pears   **e** bananas to oranges   **f** oranges to bananas

2 Read the recipe to find out which two fruits are being compared in each of these ratios. Then write each ratio using the symbol.

    a 4 to 2   **b** 4 to 1   **c** 3 to 1   **d** 1 to 2   **e** 3 to 4

3 Look at the recipe for Fruit Punch. Write the ratio you would use to compare the quantities of each two ingredients.

    a pineapple juice to soda water

    b soda water to ginger ale

    c ginger ale to soda water

    d oranges to limes

    e limes to strawberries

    f strawberries to limes

    g oranges to lemons

    h lemons to oranges

FRUIT PARTY PUNCH

3 l	pineapple juice
4 l	dry ginger ale
2 l	soda water
8	oranges (juiced)
8	lemons (juiced)
3	limes (juiced)
12	strawberries (quartered)
10	mint leaves

Can we compare the quantity of pineapple juice with the quantity of oranges?

No, we can't compare quantities when the unit of measurement is not the same.

Litres and pieces of fruit are different units of measurement.

Chris and Jane were investigating the measurements of coins.

The one-pound coin has a mass of 10 g.

The distance across the coin is about 22 mm.

For the coins that are circles we call the 'distance across' the *diameter*.

They wrote their measurements on a chart.

COINS			
Coin	Mass	Width or diameter	Thickness
£1	10 g	22 mm	3 mm
50p			

1 **Find the mass, width and thickness of all the other coins. Record your information on a chart like this.**

2 **Suppose you had these quantities of one-pound coins.**

● 10   ● 50   ● 150   ● 250

a What is the value of each quantity of coins?

b What is the mass of each quantity of coins?

c What is the length of each quantity of coins placed end-to-end?

3 **How many of each of these coins would you need to make £100?**

a £1   b 10p   c 1p   d 50p   e 20p   f 2p

4 **Suppose you had £100 worth of each type of coin.**

● £1   ● 10p   ● 1p   ● 50p   ● 20p   ● 2p

a For each type of coin, what is the total mass of £100 worth?

b What is the total length of a row made from one of each type of coin?

5 **Compare your results from Question 4.**
What is the difference between:

a the lightest and the heaviest £100 worth of coins

b the longest and the shortest row?

Jan and Craig timed each other to see how many skips they could do in one minute.

I'll count my skips.

I will stop you after one minute.

Skips in 1 minute

Jan   47 skips
Craig   39 skips

1 If Jan kept up her rate, how many skips could she do in:

 a 2 minutes   b 3 minutes   c 4 minutes   d 5 minutes   e 10 minutes?

2 If Craig kept up his rate, how many skips could he do in:

 a 2 minutes   b 4 minutes   c 6 minutes   d 10 minutes   e 20 minutes?

Shahid and Fatima wanted to time each other to see how many 3-digit numbers they could write per minute. They timed each other for 5 minutes and then worked out their approximate rates per minute.

I'll start writing at 100 and stop when you tell me to.

Then we'll need to divide by 5 to find out how many we would average each minute.

We'll call that our rate per minute.

Rate per minute
Shahid   48 numbers
Fatima   43 numbers

3 How many numbers did each child write in 5 minutes?

4 If Shahid kept up his rate per minute, how many numbers could he write in:

 a 3 minutes   b 6 minutes   c 10 minutes   d 15 minutes   e 20 minutes?

5 If Fatima kept up her rate per minute, what is the approximate time it would take her to reach 999?

6 Use Shahid and Fatima's method to work out your own rate per minute for:

 a skips   b writing 3-digit numbers   c steps around the playground.

Mrs Bourner's class set up an experiment to investigate the rates at which water drips through holes of different sizes.

We'll use 2 identical containers and prick a different-sized hole in the bottom of each.

We'll have to make sure both holes are small enough to make the water drip.

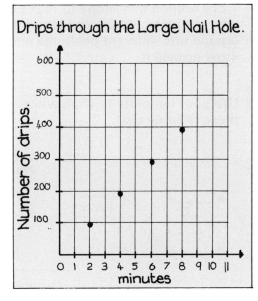

Drips through the Large Nail Hole.

Celia and Jeff tried out the container with the larger hole. They plotted points on a graph to show their results for 2, 4, 6 and 8 minutes.

(2, 98)   (4, 196)   (6, 294)   (8, 392)

1 **For each point on the graph, divide the number of drips by the number of minutes.**

  a What answer did you get each time?

  b What was the rate per minute?

2 **Copy the graph on a piece of paper.**

  a Plot these missing points which will show the number of drips for:

   ● 1 minute   ● 3 minutes   ● 5 minutes   ● 7 minutes   ● 10 minutes.

  b What do you notice about the points?

Charlie and Zoe tried out the container with the smaller hole. These are the results they got for 3, 6 and 9 minutes.   (3, 84)   (6, 168)   (9, 252)

3 **Make a graph to show the results of Charlie and Zoe's try.**

  a Plot their results on the graph.

  b Plot the missing points to show the number of drips there would be for:

   ● 2 minutes   ● 4 minutes   ● 5 minutes   ● 8 minutes   ● 10 minutes.

  c What was the rate per minute?

4 **Do your own experiment with two containers, each with a different-sized hole pricked in the bottom. Each time:**

  a Count and record the number of drips for

   ● 2 minutes   ● 3 minutes   ● 5 minutes.

  b Record the rate per minute.

The pupils in Miss Neale's class were investigating patterns and symmetry. They made lots of different patterns by repeating the same shape in different positions.
Ali drew around his cardboard shape eight times to make this design.

1 Trace around this shape to make your own template. Move your template around into different positions and draw around it.

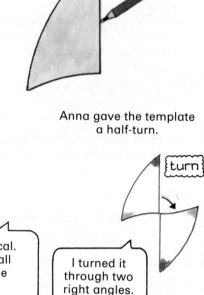

2 Use your template to copy what these children did.

Sam slid the template along.

Sue flipped the template over to the other side.

Anna gave the template a half-turn.

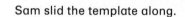 {slide}

 {flip}

{turn}

> The pairs of matching corners are all the same distance apart.

> My new shape is symmetrical. The matching corners are all the same distance from the line of symmetry.

> I turned it through two right angles.

a

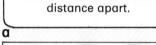

b

c

3 Look at the patterns a, b and c on this page and try to decide:
- which pattern uses a slide? . . . a flip? . . . a turn?
- which pattern uses two or more of these movements?

4 Make a template of another shape and use it to design some different patterns. Talk about the symmetries in your patterns.

Group A did a survey of the class and wrote a tally of all the shoe sizes.

Size	1	2	3	4	5	6	7	8	9	10
			II	IIII	IIII III	IIII III	II	I		

Group B used Group A's survey and made a frequency table to show how often each size occurred.

Size	1	2	3	4	5	6	7	8	9	10
	0	0	2	4	5	6	2	1	0	0

Group C used the survey data and made a pictogram with paper cut-outs.

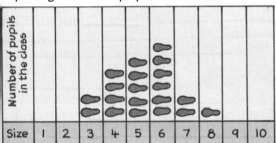

Group D made a bar graph and discussed the results.

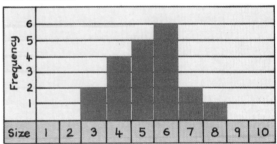

1 **Look at each display.**

a How many pupils took part in the survey?

b Which sizes did not occur in the survey at all?

c Which size occurred most frequently?

d Which size occurred least frequently?

e What was the range of shoe sizes in the class?

f Which display gave you the best idea of the results?

The most frequently occurring score or measurement is known as the *mode*.

2 Use the frequency table to help you decide how many pairs of skates in each size you would order for a group of 200 pupils of the same age.

3 Choose different ways to display information about the shoe sizes in your class. Use your displays to help you find the mode for your class.

© 1992 Schofield & Sims Limited

0 7217 2414 0

All rights reserved.

No part of this publication may be
reproduced, stored in a retrieval system, or
transmitted in any form or by any means,
electronic, mechanical, photocopying,
recording, or otherwise, without the prior
permission of Schofield & Sims Ltd.

First printed 1992

Many of the ideas and concepts embodied in
Maths Quest are derived from *Moving into
Maths* published by Moving into Maths Pty Ltd,
Melbourne, Australia.

Design, Artwork and Typesetting by PFB Design and Print Consultants, Leeds
Printed in Scotland by Scotprint Limited, Musselburgh